THE EDUCATION UTILITY

THE POWER TO REVITALIZE
EDUCATION AND SOCIETY

The Education Utility

THE POWER TO REVITALIZE EDUCATION AND SOCIETY

Dennis D. Gooler

Dean, College of Education
Northern Illinois University

Educational Technology Publications
Englewood Cliffs, New Jersey 07632

Library of Congress Cataloging-in-Publication Data

Gooler, Dennis D.
 The education utility.

 Bibliography: p.
 Includes index.
 1. Education–United States–Data processing.
 2. Computer managed instruction–United States.
 3. Computer-assisted instruction–United States.
 4. School management and organization–United States–
 Data processing. I. Title.
 LB1028.43.G66   1986   371.3'9445   86-80310
 ISBN 0-87778-205-9

Printed in the United States of America.

Library of Congress Catalog Card Number:
86-80310.

International Standard Book Number:
0-87778-205-9.

First Printing: June, 1986.

To Karen

Whose love and support, as well as professional
contributions made this writing possible

and Jack

Whose vision and persistence
got the journey underway.

FOREWORD

As a society, we are attempting to respond to certain critical issues: economic challenges, international tensions, threats to family cohesion, social inequities, addictions and abuses.

Our efforts are reminiscent of the doctor who said, "I feel like I'm pulling people out of the river and giving them mouth-to-mouth resuscitation. It's happening so fast, I don't have time to go upriver to see who's pushing them in."

Where do we get "pushed into" the river of confused competition? Where did we learn the fear of being wrong? Where does our self-esteem first become shaky?

There is a place where we took on the numbing sense of personal limits, where we labeled ourselves and each other, where we learned to fake it.

You know the place. We call it school.

And it was nobody's fault. Not the people who dreamed of mass education for literacy, not the people who tried to design an assembly-line system. They did their best, given the time and the tools. We should honor them.

But we are now paying the very great price for an educational system that has not kept apace of our need for a society of well-educated individuals-confident, responsible thinkers and doers. People who can assume personal leadership in a complex age when no designated leader can give us all the answers.

Our problems are not beyond solving. They are beyond our present methods. And as Einstein put it, you can never solve a problem at the level on which you created it.

Reform of education has always fallen short of renewal. Schools have been our ideological battlegrounds, as factions fought for more or less structure, more or less discipline, more or fewer options. And no one has been satisfied.

A concept called the Education Utility may turn out to be the lever for a recommitment to learning. The Utility is a delivery system for an immense, rich, sophisticated array of information resources. It offers educators and the community a chance to redesign education nearer to the heart's desire. The technology offers not only instruction but empowerment. We become trained in the use of instruments that can serve us in a dynamic, complex age. The technology brings us processing power . . . the capacity to simulate . . . electronic mail . . . data-base access . . . information management systems.

By giving talented educators, software designers, and others the opportunity to create individualized interactive instruction and administrative support systems, the Education Utility will make it easier for teachers to educate — to draw out the uniqueness of each person.

The Education Utility concept has attracted the help of some remarkable people. Dennis Gooler, who acknowledges them in this book, is himself one of the most remarkable. When he learned about the Utility, he was so excited but cautious; like everyone who cares deeply about education, he had been disappointed before by large-scale solutions. He liked the answers he got from people at AT&T and National Information Utilities Corporation (including "we don't know yet"). And he offered to help find solutions.

Dennis Gooler's way of finding solutions is to sound the call for help. Let the cream of our society's talent — educators, communicators, healers, artists, scientists — join forces for a renaissance to be catalyzed by this collaboration. And let us each call on our own best to solve our most central problem: the need to become better problem-solvers. Let this be the beginning of the Age of Intelligence.

Scientists have proven that the human brain is profoundly flexible and self-teaching. Experiments have shown that the normal child, given the right training and stimulation, is capable of what we consider giftedness. But this innate genius cannot flower in boredom or fear.

We can put what we know to work. There already exists a budding expertise to enhance intelligence, to teach clear thinking, to train attention and recovery from mistakes. We can take advantage of state-of-the-art knowledge to train children and ourselves.

The time has come to go beyond coping. Working together, we can create an educational environment that will excite us. We can take artful use of these new tools for our liberation.

The Education Utility or a similar concept is a necessary but not sufficient ingredient for the change. It will only work if all elements of the society play a healthy creative and corrective role. No one organization can take on such a large task alone. If we want to be alive in the Age of Intelligence, it has to become the new American dream — our national agenda and our national adventure.

Marilyn Ferguson
Author, *The Aquarian Conspiracy*

PREFACE

In the summer of 1985, I was invited to present a paper at an international convention in Vancouver, British Columbia. The convention, on teacher education, drew participants from countries throughout the world. After checking in with the conference, I took a few minutes to find out what was on the program. I noted a keynote presentation, on the "Education Utility," to be delivered by someone named Jack Taub. The brief annotation noted the Education Utility was a new application of technology in education that could be important for teacher education. Having chaired a department of instructional technology for some years, and now dean of a large College of Education, I was interested in topics that involved technology with education.

Taub turned in quite a performance. The Education Utility was a fascinating topic, but my real fascination was with Taub himself. He conveyed a spirit of evangelism at the Utility presentation. Taub clearly was sold on his dream for a new society, the roles education could play in that society, and the need for schools to be exciting places for young people. He made no apologies for his enthusiasm. He argued that education was tired and that the Education Utility was the tonic it needed. He talked about individualizing education in ways that only someone outside the education establishment could envision. He argued that the Utility could create the "Age of Intelligence." Taub said a student's desk ought to be a kind of "intellectual Disneyland." Teachers using the Utility will, in fact, be able to deal effectively with individual differences and needs across the curricular areas. He observed that the Utility could help address issues of equity, urban education, integrating higher order thinking skills into the school curriculum, and other challenges.

Taub had the audacity to promise that the extraordinary could become commonplace. We in the establishment knew better; we'd been there before, with a variety of technology fixes and had discovered that individualized education played well in theory but did not translate into practice. To be sure, Taub's description of the Utility sounded both novel and attractive, but I, like so many others in the education business for a while, was cynical. Still, there was something different here. . . .

Later that evening, I saw Taub sitting in the lobby, introduced myself to him, and told Taub I was intrigued by his concept of the Utility, but that, in my judgment, his system was not likely to work unless teachers and administrators were prepared adequately to use the Utility. I argued that other vendors of magical technologies seemed to slight this preparation factor and as a result, technologies were seldom, if ever, successfully integrated into the instructional strategies of teachers. What, I asked, is *your* Utility going to do about this?

Taub's response was simple: "I've thought about this problem," he said, "but I don't have any clear answers. Why don't *you* help us?" I wasn't quite prepared for that response; those of us in academics are more prone to raising questions than supplying answers. But I *did* think about the matter. Early the next morning, I found a typewriter and wrote a few pages about how to prepare people to use the Education Utility. I gave Taub the brief paper and invited his comments. He seemed surprised at the prompt response to his offer. Later that day, we met again, this time with his associate, Paul Geffert, and talked some more.

Thus began what has become for me an exciting and professionally stimulating experience. After learning as much about the Education Utility idea as I could, I volunteered to help move the idea along. A proposal was developed for a conference of college of education deans to discuss the Utility in general and what implications the Utility might have for teacher preparation programs. From that conference came other exciting prospects. At one point I suggested to Taub that it might be useful to pull together some of the many ideas being discussed about the educational implications of the Utility. He asked if I would do the pulling together. This book is the result — an attempt to document some of the preliminary thinking about the implementation of the Education Utility.

Before sharing this thinking with you, I want to provide a bit more background on the people I've come to know through the Education Utility concept. First, Taub is a truly unique individual; he is a missionary; he believes deeply in providing quality individualized education for everyone, and is passionately committed to his approach to realizing his dream. This cause, and the concept of the Utility itself, has very personal roots. Taub's son has cerebral palsy. He had the fortunate opportunity to receive quality educational experiences, largely through individualized programs of study developed for him by special education personnel. Taub saw the positive impact individualized programs had on his son and wondered (naively, of course) why such programs couldn't be available for everyone. He set out on a journey to make it happen. He has invested enormous personal resources on his journey. As a founder and largest individual stockholder of The Source, the nation's first information utility, Taub had a sense about providing access to information; he believes that schools should provide unlimited access for students to information, on an individualized basis. So the Utility was born not out of just a dream, but from a *practical* base in experience and know-how. Taub is tireless in tracking down ideas. I know; I have received my share of 3 a.m. telephone calls from him. He does not have all the answers and sometimes does not have a comprehensive sense of exactly how the education system works. But this is precisely why Taub is so very much needed; he doesn't carry some of the historical baggage about education that so many of us do. He doesn't know why certain things can't be done.

I have met others who share Taub's vision. Paul Geffert, the Senior Vice President of National Information Utilities Corporation (of which Taub is chairman), brings keen insights to the Utility project with a background in education, journalism, and public affairs. I have found him to be intellectually stimulating, competent, and with personal values consistent with the positive goals held for the Utility. Geffert keeps the wheels moving.

AT&T's decision to become the major corporate partner in the Education Utility was, of course, an extremely important development. The prospects for success of the Utility increased significantly with AT&T's involvement. The people in leadership roles for the Utility are first rate talents. Mike Landau's calm, steady, but enthusiastic involvement in the project has been absolutely instrumental in bringing the Utility to where it is today. Rick Peters, responsible for many of the AT&T Information Systems projects in education, has a unique and valuable insight on both education and business. Peters knows how to ask the tough questions but is also willing to look for answers. Dave Atkinson moved the project along with a hard-headed understanding of and commitment to the Utility concept. There are numerous other people within AT&T and the National Information

Utilities Corporation who are making major contributions to both the conceptual and practical aspects of "rolling out" the Education Utility. AT&T, one of the largest American corporations, has an opportunity in this venture to provide real leadership for technological applications in education. AT&T could serve as a kind of international lightening rod for new ideas on educational and social improvements, a magnificent role for an American corporation.

But there is more to this story. The groundswell of interest in and participation by people all over the nation who sense in the Education Utility an important idea grows continuously. People are volunteering their time to write papers, attend meetings, and plan projects related to the Utility. In the 20 years I have been in the education field, I have seen nothing quite like this. It is as though educators and interested citizens have been waiting for some optimistic event, some idea that is positive and forward looking, to shake them out of what can most kindly be called educational doldrums. The numerous national reports of the past several years have told us what we are not doing well, but few, if any, of those reports have provided truly innovative leadership. The Education Utility offers a very pragmatic brand of hope, coupled with a plan of action. Perhaps that is why the Utility idea is generating the kind of response it is: we are anxious to do better, to create better education and a better society. We are eager to work together on ideas that make sense. The Education Utility represents an important step in our efforts to harness modern technology for the good of education.

I am one of those individuals who have found excitement and hope in the Utility concept. I have been too long in higher education to be without caution in these matters, considering the prior technologies proclaimed as the answer to all our education problems. The Education Utility is not without difficulties, but at some point one needs to decide what is important and give it a best shot. I don't know if the Utility will be all that it is claimed to be, but I am sure no new approaches to improving education and society will work unless some of us pitch in and help. Those in key positions to develop and implement the Utility have invited educators to be a part of the development process, which in itself is something of a novel approach. We, as educators, ought to take advantage of the opportunity and see if we can make a difference in our society.

Finally, a brief word about this book and my involvement with it. I have never tried to write anything quite like this before. The book is certainly not classic academic scholarship but it is rather a kind of "before-the-fact" analysis of a future educational phenomenon.

It is an attempt to weave together some exciting possibilities with some hard realities. More than anything, this is meant to stimulate the imagination, to create in readers a sense of excitement about what might be and an interest in being a participant in what could very well be a dramatic and influential intervention in how we educate our citizenry. Perhaps the book will be influential in shaping the future of the Utility, or in the decisions of those considering whether to invest in the Utility for their schools or other educational agencies. I will be satisfied if this volume sets readers thinking about how we can make the tools of our emerging information society better serve our learning needs.

It is important to say I have written this book as a private individual. I have not been employed or retained by AT&T or by the National Information Utilities Corporation. Personnel in both corporations have cooperated fully in my attempts to gather information about the Utility but have not themselves written any of the book. Furthermore, the ideas presented in this volume may or may not be entirely consistent with the thinking of officials in the two corporations. Throughout, I and others who have contributed to the book suggest how the Utility should be developed. I have written this because I think the Education Utility idea is terribly important, one that has great promise and one that deserves to be fully tried. I am convinced that if the Utility does succeed, we will all be the better for it. I am equally convinced that success will depend largely on the willingness and capacity of the education system to be full participants in planning and implementing the idea.

Taub has said to me on a number occasions that he believes we have the need, the motivation, the technology, the know-how, and the resources to make the Utility happen. If it fails, it will be because we fumbled the concept, and it will be our own fault. I think he is right.

My thanks to those who made contributions to this volume, as noted throughout the text. They include:

Peter Abrams, Northern Illinois University;
Karen Brown, Northern Illinois University;
Brian Cahill, AT&T Information Systems;
Carol Carrier, University of Minnesota;
Fred Frank, Northern Illinois University;
Arden Grotelueschen, Grotelueschen Associates;
Ken Komoski, Educational Products Information Exchange;
Jack Kosiorek, AT&T Information Systems;

John McLevie, University of Houston at Clear Lake;
Muriel Mackett, Northern Illinois University;
Jeri Nowakowski, Northern Illinois University;
Annette Paperello, Shoreham-Wading River Central School District;
Carol Passavant, AT&T Information Systems;
Mike Sullivan, Maryland Instructional Television; and
Walter Yatko, AT&T Information Systems.

They, too, have been volunteers in this venture. In the end, however, I stand responsible for errors of fact or inappropriateness of conclusions.

Dennis D. Gooler
January, 1986

TABLE OF CONTENTS

THE EDUCATION UTILITY

THE POWER TO REVITALIZE
EDUCATION AND SOCIETY

CHAPTER ONE

AMERICA, PART TWO: THE JOURNEY BEGINS

There are two predictions to which I would assign a high probability of value. The first is that people who do not educate themselves — and keep reeducating themselves — to participate in the new knowledge environment will be the peasants of the information society. The second is that societies that do not give all their people an opportunity for relevant education, as well as periodic opportunities to fine tune their knowledge and their insights, will be left in the jet stream of history by those that do.

Harlan Cleveland (1985)

This volume is about a journey, one different from what the reader finds in travel sections of the Sunday papers.

Journeys, both actual and metaphorical, always have been a significant part of the landscape of human experience. Our literature is rich with the chronicling of journeys. We read in Homer of the journey of Odysseus and other characters. Jonathan Swift brought us the travels of Gulliver. Coleridge shared with us the journey of the ancient mariner. DeToqueville toured America and wrote of what he saw and thought of this new democracy. Paul Theroux writes about the world as a collection of journeys. Very recently, William Least Heat Moon took us on a journey across America, over the blue highways of his roadmap. We always have been captivated by journeys.

They convey newness, excitement, the chance to experience the unusual. Journeys bring new beginnings, new hopes and sometimes new fears. *Travel* may become routine to those whose business it is to travel; *journeys*, however, are never routine nor boring because they quest for things beyond ourselves. Journeys renew the senses, sharpen resolve, and bring new perspectives to our daily lives. Those who embark on journeys, who are explorers, rarely return unchanged from a journey. Because of our journeys, we become renewed.

Journeys not yet taken are called dreams, visions of a future that might be. Journeys and dreams sometimes are indistinguishable from one another, particularly as journeys are being planned. Just as our literature and our history document journeys, so too do science fiction, futurist writing, and utopian imaginings provide a literature of our dreams and our visions. This literature records journeys we want to take, dreams we either fear or hope for. Dreams are, in many respects, our goals or targets for the future. Journeys are what propel us toward those goals.

This Itinerary

This is a volume about a particular dream and about the journey that just has begun to pursue it. On one level, the dream is simple: to create a learning society that makes it possible for all of us through education, to achieve what we want to become and what a just society needs in an educated citizenry. The dream simply is to make learning possible, desirable, enjoyable and affordable for all of us throughout our lives. The fundamental premises of this dream also are relatively simple: learning is vital to the well-being of every individual; learned and learning people are essential for a just and reasonable society; we have both the resources and the technologies to create a learning society; and we should get on about the task of making it happen. This dream also encompasses two corollary assumptions: that it is desirable to tailor a learning system to meet the needs of *individuals*, as well as groups; and that it now is *possible* to accomplish individualized education in a meaningful and efficient manner.

This dream for a learning society does not belong to any single individual nor any particular time in history. In the United States, and indeed throughout the world, visionaries long have imagined a society in which all could avail themselves of lifetime learning opportunities. The ordinary person, say these visionaries, ought to have access to the information of the world, irrespective of social or economic status or age. The fate of any society ultimately rests in the hands and minds of its citizens and in their ability to better themselves continuously through learning. Such has been the dream of many people for many centuries. To be sure, there were (and are) those who contend not all people *could* or *should* learn. And occasionally it appears to some that our education system reflects this view. For the most part, however, the United States can be proud of its education system, despite the criticisms leveled against it, because few other nations have achieved the level of general education attained in this country. But even here, we fall far short of the visionary view of a learning society.

And surely there will be those who find the energy of the Utility protagonists to be only so much empty optimism. There are those who will see only the reasons why things cannot be done and will not dream of the reasons why things *should* be done. The fashionable pessimists will find plenty to criticize. But with any luck, a certain optimism *will* prevail, and enough people will join the journey to give the effort a fair chance to succeed. As more and more people see the outline of an idea in the Education Utility, they will contribute their creative talents to help give the idea some body. The Education Utility, if it is to make a difference in society, in making the world a better place for all of us, will do so because we are willing to believe that the world *can* be made better through the maturation of a learning society, and that just maybe the Education Utility is setting off in the right direction. John Gardner (1963), in his book *Self-Renewal*, provides a fitting benediction to this description of the start of a journey:

> The capacity of our people to believe stubbornly and irrepressibly that this is a world worth saving, and that intelligence and energy and good will might save it, is one of the most endearing and bracing of American traits. . . . No sensible person relishes the immature aspects of our optimism but if we lose that optimism we will surely be a less spirited people, a less magnanimous people and an immeasurably less venturesome people. Zest and generosity will disappear from our national style. And our impact on the world may well disappear along with them. (p. 114)

The Education Utility is thus something of a dream, a concept based on some laudable goals for our society. But the Utility is also a very concrete technology that must be effectively operated by users if the dream is to be translated into practical reality. Chapter Two contains a description of how the Education Utility will actually work.

As with many dreams held *for* a society in general, *by* a society in general, dreams remain only dreams unless or until individuals or groups embark on journeys designed to translate those dreams into reality. This volume describes the beginnings of one such journey, initially undertaken by a single person, and subsequently joined by other individuals, organizations, and corporations convinced that the journey is worth taking. Begun 10 years ago, that journey has taken shape and direction and acquired a name: *The Education Utility* (TM)*. The Education Utility is a journey about education and learning, but it also is about a more general concern for the very character of our future society.

In his marvelous book, *The Discoverers*, Daniel Boorstin (1983) describes the need felt by human beings to bring some order to their lives:

> So long as man marked his life only by the cycles of nature — the changing seasons, the waxing or waning moon — he remained a prisoner of nature. If he was to go his own way and fill his world with human novelties, he would have to make his own measures of time. . . . . The week — or something very like it — was probably the earliest of these artificial time clusters. But the week is no Western invention, nor has it everywhere been a cluster of seven days. . . . . What is planet-wide is not any particular bouquet of days but the need and desire to make some kind of bouquet. Mankind has revealed a potent, pressing desire to play with time, to make more of it than nature has made. (pp. 12-13)

As is the case with measures of time, we tend to divide our history into ages, stages, periods, or categories. Depending on the particular segment of history being considered, the labels change. We speak of the Ice Age, the Industrial Revolution, the Age of Reason, the Renaissance, the Dark Ages, the boom times, the Depression. We divide time and events into categories which we can label so that we can bring some understandable order to the flow of human events. Our categories are largely arbitrary, highlighting a dramatic event here and there, but they often help us to better understand our past and envision our future.

America, Part Two

Another dividing of the flow of history is proposed in this volume. We as a nation stand poised on the edge of a new label, *America, Part Two*. This dramatically signals the start of a fundamentally new period in our society. *America, Part Two* hints at the closing of an incredibly rich and varied age and the start of a new age, rooted in the continuity of history but whose problems, processes, and products may be substantially different.

* *The Education Utility* is a registered trademark of National Information Utilities Corporation.

This *America, Part Two* will feature broad advances in the integration of the myriad separate technologies, enterprises and values that characterize our present society.

In *America, Part Two* we will learn to put the critical pieces of society together to create environments truly conducive to advancing mankind. We will rebuild the basic infrastructure of society by harnessing together information, technology, and human creativity.

This age will not be without problems or shortcomings, but in *America, Part Two* we can come closer than ever before to creating a society that represents the best of what humanity can be because at the core it will be a genuine learning society.

Why draw a line now, why declare the end of one age and the beginning of a new period? Of course, categories really can be drawn only after the fact, as historians seek to characterize a period of time. But the concept of *America, Part Two* is perhaps best understood as a dream, a declaration of possibility and intent, rather than a chronicling of historical events. *America, Part Two* is a statement about what we can *choose* to do with and about our collective future and, as such, serves as a blueprint for action and a call for undertaking significant journeys. *America, Part Two* is worth considering, however, not because it is a dream, but because it is a *possible* dream, quite within our grasp with what we already know and have and what we will yet discover.

It might be said of our time that America has reached a plateau in its development. The nation has become technologically complex in a comparatively short time. We wrestle with new, fundamental problems, including tensions among those representing different cultural experiences and aspirations; a national economy failing to meet the basic needs of millions of citizens; an ambivalence about the nation's place in the world; the constant threat of nuclear holocaust; confusion about the roles of basic social institutions; changes in basic family structures; and for many, apathy and lack of antici-pation. Yet, in the midst of these problems we see optimism about the future. The early 1980s already have been characterized by some as a time in which we have begun to balance high technology opportunities with the need to attend to the human dimensions of living. Many people have a vague sense of things not being quite right but also are uncertain of either the causes of this unrest or the proper solutions to the problems. People look for causes in the nation's school system, in the justice system, and, perhaps less often, in themselves.

Americans always have sought direct answers to issues, and no less so as we reach the beginning of a new era. One difference, of course, is that Americans no longer can define solutions only for themselves. It is clear we live in a global community, like it or not. Our telecommunications and transportation triumphs make it virtually impossible to isolate ourselves within our geographic boundaries.

How Will It Be Different?

The time is right for America to enter the next phase of social development. What ought to be its character, this *America, Part Two*? What ought the dream to include?

It is clear that during *America, Part Two* we must encourage the building of a rich and diverse society, drawing on the vast cultural richness brought by those who come from distant places. We must learn and respect the value of cultural pluralism, no longer forcing everyone into a common mold.

We must also discover new and more effective ways of engaging people in self-governance, to refute the impersonality of government bureaucracies. We recognize with new meaning the notion that we *are* the government, and that we have a responsibility to govern ourselves.

Another key characteristic of *America, Part Two* is that our nation must commit itself strongly to the cultural and intellectual development of our citizens. We must declare that it is unacceptable to have large numbers of our adults illiterate. We need to acknowledge more clearly the work and importance of those committed to our intellectual growth, renewing our support for teachers and teaching and learning.

And perhaps at the most general level, we must regain a sense of personal and community connectedness. We must make choices in our allocation of resources that will empower and enrich human lives. It seems absurd to single out this characteristic as being worthy of special mention for we might assume that, *of course*, this is a characteristic of any society. Yet, for some time many have felt a loss of personal control in a society grown unbearably complex. Some are fearful and unconnected to anything or anyone. This may be changed in *America, Part Two*.

We can learn more fully to integrate the discrete components of our society. We can align our education and employment systems. We can bring our health care, judicial, and social systems together to deal with the wholeness of individual human beings. We even can achieve compatibility among our technological innovations, making it much easier to create *systems* of technologies that work *for* us. We can achieve a greater balance between "high tech and high touch." Our institutions will work more effectively for us, in part by improving every individual's access, through our technologies, to other people and ideas that matter. We also can reorient our workplaces and retool our workforce to be more productive and more satisfied with its work. There are never enough resources, of course, but we can make better use of what we have. We can make a commitment to reducing technological obsolescence. And we can restore the nation's education system to the cornerstone of society, acknowledging the centrality of learning to the development of a stable and just society.

Education In America, Part Two

It is with this last point that the Education Utility is primarily concerned: the enhancement of the education system and the goal of becoming a learning society. If we are on the threshold of a new era, then surely education and learning will be even more vital to the future described as *America, Part Two.* The Education Utility journey begins at a time of potentially high consequence for education in this country. During the past several years, the education system has undergone intense scrutiny. We have been told, through the reports of various individuals and organizations, that we are a nation at risk, our schools are not doing the job, our colleges are not adequately preparing new teachers, our standards are too low. These examinations and conclusions arise from widespread suspicion that all is not right, that our education system is seriously declining. There is concern for the future of our education institutions and our ability to prepare future generations to function effectively in society.

Predictably, state after state has joined the movement for educational reform. Major legislation enacted in state capitals around the nation calls for a variety of actions to improve the quality of education offered citizens. The full impact of these reforms remains to be seen, of course, but there is no question the public has put education back on the national agenda, if only briefly. There appears to be a hunger of sorts, a strong desire to find answers to what for many is a frustrating situation. People express a strong *belief* in the importance of education and learning but too often feel disappointed by the education *system.* Some want a quick, inexpensive fix to the problem. More thoughtful citizens see the fallacy of the quick fix and wonder if there are not more lasting ways to improve the quality of what we learn, how we learn it and what we do with what we learn.

Various forms of technology have been advocated to solve the problems of an inadequate education system. Technology, long hovering at the edges of education, is taking new forms, and finally seems poised to embrace, in a meaningful way, the education efforts of our society.

There is something new to all this. It is not just video, and our hopes for educational salvation through television. It is not just microcomputers, our latest hope. It is not just better telecommunications or insights into instructional strategies or school accountability. It is not any *single* technology that defines our hopes for the future, but rather a *combination*, an *integration* of these heretofore largely unconnected technologies that represents promise. It is not only the possession of an enlarged research base about how people learn *but* the development of new technological combinations *and* the willingness of some entrepreneurial individuals to take risks, pushing together, that may permit us to evolve to a new level of educational thought and practice.

One of these individuals, Jack Taub, founder of the Education Utility, with a few friends sharing a vision for and intense interest in helping shape a learning society based on a new generation of technology, took some risks and started a journey.

Taub once observed:

> The fragmentary way in which computer products and certain media have been pushed upon the schools in recent years has caused confusion and frustration. There is a growing anxiety among administrators and teachers that microcomputers in the classroom are not delivering the instructional advantages promised by the hardware manufacturers. Anticipating this problem, National Information Utilities Corporation recognized that it would only be a matter of time before teachers and administrators realized that the uncoordinated introduction of educational technologies into the classroom could not work to satisfactory levels of learning, productivity and efficiency. Taking these problems into account, NIU set out to develop a cost effective operating system that integrates four major media components — computing, software, information, and telecommunications — with the various support services essential to exploiting fully their instructional potential.

The Education Utility signals the start of new ways to conceptualize and deliver educational opportunities for young and old alike in this country and throughout the world. The Education Utility is first and foremost an idea about how to enrich education, and only secondarily a technological system. It begins by raising fundamental questions about content, strategies, and purposes of instruction and then provides answers to those tough questions. The Education Utility is not meant to be an add on to strategies used to teach and learn, but rather an integral, integrated aspect of those strategies. It is not a substitute for teachers, but rather a tool and a set of resources that will empower teachers to teach in the most effective and stimulating ways possible. The Utility will alleviate many of the burdensome administrative/bookkeeping tasks from teachers.

The Education Utility is a resource of unparalleled power for the individual learner who will be able to access information and ideas in ways never thought feasible. The Education Utility is meant to open the doors to the world's information resources, for every individual learner, as well as provide a means for learners to connect with each other, creating a true learning society. Richard Niebuhr (1984), in his book *Revitalizing American Learning*, captured the essence of the concept underlying the Education Utility:

> The new learning model rediscovers some ancient truths about the human species: human learning is instrumental to goals; it occurs in many settings; and it has many modes. The adjustments required of us as individuals and of our mainstream institutions are modest and do not require vast expenditures. But they do require that we replace our present concept of education with a new understanding of human learning. (p.6)

Achieving a culturally rich society that also is just and economically fair to all citizens is no small goal, nor will the goal be accomplished by any single intervention, event, person, or time period. But we can make a start, and education is a logical place to begin. We can join a journey just begun to reach these lofty but crucial goals.

How Will It Work?

Just what is the Education Utility? Why have so many individuals, organizations and institutions become enamored with its potential to enhance the quality of learning? This volume is a response to these kinds of questions. In Chapter Two, for example, the reader is offered a detailed description of what the Education Utility is and how it works. But a few introductory and descriptive remarks may be in order here.

The Education Utility is an electronic delivery and management system that will provide instantly, to the desks of educators and students located anywhere in the world, massive quantities of continually updated instructionally interactive information (software programs, databases, sophisticated graphics capabilities, news services, electronic journals, electronic mail, and other instructional and administrative materials). All of these materials will be stored or accessed through a main "host" computer. Individual educational sites (school buildings, etc.) will be connected via a state network to that main host or Network Control Center, through whatever communications channels are most easily and inexpensively available. Each education site will have a special site-based computer, permitting storage of any of the materials or services the local site wishes to obtain from the control center. Those materials will be transmitted directly (and at off-hours when transmission costs are lowest) from the network control center at the request of teachers and administrators at the local site.

Each instructional setting (such as an individual classroom) at the local site will also have a storage and switching device, connected to the site-based storage computer. Up to 30 microcomputers will be connected to the classroom level storage device, enabling 30 microcomputers to be simultaneously working on up to 30 different programs. Teachers thus will be able to truly individualize education programs for all students, while maintaining the capacity for groups of students to work together. In addition, the Utility will permit students to communicate with other students, within a local area, a nation, or, indeed, anywhere in the world, through electronic, inexpensive mail. Furthermore, teachers and administrators will have available a full range of administrative management and communication tools via the Utility.

The Utility will provide instructional programs and strategies never before possible. And, of course, the Utility will provide opportunities for continuing professional education and general instructional support to teachers and administrators.

The Education Utility, through its integration of technologies and its vast information resources, as well as the tremendous computing power it makes available to each user, will provide for at least the following educational benefits:

1. Self-paced interaction between students and the the growing amount of knowledge to be learned;

2. Teachers relieved of some of the rote aspects of teaching, including paper work, so they can spend more time on the more rewarding and important aspects of teaching and learning;

3. True customization of instruction for all children, including children with particular learning needs and/or handicapping conditions;

4. Infinitely patient presentation of information and tireless man-

agement of routine drillwork, as well as opportunities for creative new ways of learning more complex material and concepts;

5. More *student* control of contingencies and variables in simulation exercises;
6. Realtime "windows on the world" through ready access to information available in electronic mail, databases, videotapes, and instructional television from around the world;
7. Opportunities to provide comprehensive understandings of the cultures of other peoples of the world;
8. A viable means to locate, retrieve, manage, and store the information products of the knowledge explosion;
9. A way for teachers and administrators to better manage their workloads;
10. An efficient means to upgrade the preparation of current teachers and administrators and to initially prepare, in conjunction with local higher education institutions, the thousands of new teachers and administrators needed in the future; and
11. A way of more effectively preparing young people for meaningful employment.

The Education Utility thus represents an important and potentially powerful aspect of the kind of new learning and education system described by Niebuhr, a system of learning likely to characterize *America, Part Two.*

This document on the Education Utility is organized into chapters that each address an important aspect of the Education Utility:

1. Chapter Two comprehensively describes the Education Utility, including the hardware and software characteristics of the system;
2. Chapter Three includes an analysis of some of the public policy issues that may be raised by the Education Utility. Among these are issues of equity, local control, etc.;
3. Chapter Four includes a more in-depth description of how the Utility will both fit into the current educational system and how it might shape the future of that system. Included in this chapter is a discussion of the implications of the Utility for curricula and instructional strategies, the design and development of educational materials, and the administration and management of schools and other educational settings;
4. Chapter Five contains an analysis of issues related to the preparation of educators and learners in order for them to effectively use the Utility. Training will be critical to its long-term success.

This chapter includes an examination of the training needs of teachers, administrators, learners, and parents;

5. A comprehensive system for user support is planned as an integral part of the Education Utility. Chapter Six contains a description of some components that could become a part of this unusual support system, including demonstration centers, linkages with professional associations and research and development centers, general research and evaluation support, and The Academy of Learning Technologies;

6. Chapter Seven contains a brief description of ways in which the Education Utility might be used in settings other than elementary or secondary schools. Initial attention in the development of the Education Utility has been focused on applications in K-12 settings, but the Utility concept has tremendous potential in these other settings as well;

7. Chapter Eight, *The Journey Continues*, includes a very brief set of concluding remarks about the Education Utility.

Thus, the journey is begun, the challenge engaged. The Education Utility issues forth from grandiose hopes, toward noble dreams. Along the way, there will be realities in this journey. There will be successes, but so too will there be some failures. The pragmatics of business must coexist with the dreams of the visionaries. The machines will not always work as planned, and the materials may not always be as good as might be hoped. There will be those who can see no good in this technology and others who will find new worlds suddenly available for exploration. The Education Utility will provoke contrasts, as some educators will embrace the concept while others will reject it.

CHAPTER TWO

HOW THE EDUCATION UTILITY WORKS*

The initial and most fundamental question from one who hears about the Education Utility is: how does it work? This means different things, depending on who is asking the question. Some individuals want to understand in great detail how the hardware functions. Others really want a "lay person's" response; they are less concerned with how each hardware component works *technically* and more concerned with how a teacher or learner will interact with the Utility system. Variations fill the spectrum between these interests.

Chapter Two describes the workings of the Education Utility. This description lies somewhere between the extremes of possible responses to the question of how the Utility works but is somewhat closer to the non-technical than the technical end. The chapter is written as much as possible from the perspective of the average *user* of the system. Readers who desire more complete technical information on the Utility system will need to consult officials at AT&T Information Systems.

The chapter covers:

1. An overview of the Utility system;
2. A description of the hardware and software components of the system;

---

* Contributions to this chapter were made by Brian Cahill, Jack Kosiorek, Carol Passavant, and Walter Yatko, all of AT&T Informtion Systems.

3. A description of the information resources in the system;
4. One scenario of how the system will be used;
5. A description of the roles of the various partners in the Utility.

Overview

The Education Utility system is composed of a number of elements or components. Together, they form a very unique educational tool. Generally, the major features of the Education Utility include:

1. A **repository of information at the "front-end."** This information takes many forms, e.g., certain data bases; reference materials, such as encyclopedias and dictionaries; journals and magazines of various kinds; textbooks; educational software programs of all kinds; various kinds of software tools, such as word processing programs, spreadsheets, and graphics programs; and various kinds of administrative packages. This repository of information will be dynamic; that is, it will be constantly updated and expanded, depending on the needs of users of the system and on changes in data bases, educational programs, etc. Furthermore, users themselves will have opportunities to add to the repository. This collection of information, stored in computers by NIU will represent an incredible and heretofore largely unassembled and thus unavailable instructional resource for teachers and learners.

2. **Microcomputers located in individual classrooms, offices, continuing education centers, etc.** Eventually, each student in an elementary or secondary school might have a microcomputer terminal at his or her desk. At the outset, however, microcomputers hooked into the Utility probably will appear at work stations in a small number of specially designed classrooms, or in any other appropriate setting. Similarly, hospitals, continuing education centers, or other educational settings might design Utility work stations. Whatever the physical arrangement in a given setting, learners will gain access to the materials in the Utility through a microcomputer. It will hook into the Utility, and also will have significant computing power in and of itself. What is so exciting about the Utility, of course, is that each learner will be able to work with whatever information that learner needs, *when* the learner needs it. The ideal of individualized education becomes reality with the Utility system.

3. **A transmission system.** The information stored in the national computer system must be transmitted to individual schools, and, most importantly, individual student work stations. This will be accomplished through a system whereby information is transmitted from

the national computer (called the Network Control Center), via various telecommunications channels such as satellite broadcast, to a state affiliate. Information requested by a given school district or individual school then will be transmitted from the state affiliate to the district or school requesting the information, again through the most reliable and cost-effective telecommunications channels. The information will be stored at a school site computer, to be used whenever it is needed by teachers and students. Transmissions will be done during "off-hours," when telecommunications charges are lowest. Once at the school site, teachers and learners will be able to access whatever information they need, when they need it. Furthermore, those at sites away from the school (e.g., in homes, or businesses) will have access to the Utility via local telephone calls.

4. **Networking Features**. The concept of massive amounts of educational information, directly available on an individualized basis to learners and teachers, to be worked into whatever overall instructional strategies are used by the teacher, constitutes the foundation of the Education Utility. There are a number of additional features or services of the Education Utility. For example, the electronic mail or networking capacity of the Utility is a significant educational feature. Learners will be able to interact, via electronic mail, with other learners, within a classroom, school building or district, community, nation, or anywhere in the world, at a cost that is affordable. This interactive networking capability should greatly enhance the world view of learners; stress cooperative, rather than competitive learning environments; and generally increase the excitement and enjoyment of learning. No longer will learning be an isolated activity.

5. **Teacher Stations**. Another important feature of the Utility will be teacher work stations providing the means for the teacher to direct and manage all work done with the Utility. The teacher work station will contain the equipment necessary to interact with individuals or groups of students, using any program or resource contained in the Utility. The work station also will permit the teacher to monitor student progress, on an individual basis, and to complete the administrative and reporting tasks required of teachers. Ideally, the teacher work station will permit the teacher to access not only the materials available through the Utility but other materials available from cable or satellite television, film libraries, and other sources of information such as video disk, and to integrate all classroom resources.

6. **Administrative Work Stations**. These will permit school administrators to carry out administrative tasks via the Utility. The administrator will have at his or her work station a microcomputer,

connected to the Utility system. The microcomputer also will have enormous "stand-alone" computing power. The Utility will permit teachers to report to and receive from school administrators various kinds of relevant information on student progress. Administrators will have a powerful tool for aggregating and analyzing a broad range of information needed for planning, decision making, and reporting.

7. **Links With Home Stations**. The Utility also will permit linkages (as mentioned above) with home users. Learners and parents with microcomputer terminals in their homes will be able to tie into the school's Utility. Learners will be able to complete homework assignments via their home terminals. Parents will be able to communicate with teachers and administrators through the Utility and will be able to participate in adult learning as well, using the resources of the Utility.

8. **Revenue Source**. Schools will be able to sell to individuals and/ or businesses in the community excess capacity on the Utility. That is, the school can generate revenues to operate the Utility by selling time on the Utility during non-school hours to those in the community who want the information resources available through the Utility.

In sum: the Education Utility consists of a massive and dynamic reservoir of information and educational programming, from which individual teachers and learners can select the information and education resources they wish to work with, and when. The appropriate information can be transmitted via a state network in an economical manner to the school or other site requesting the information, and can be used by the individual learner as needed. Furthermore, these individualized uses of information are managed and enhanced by a number of instructional and administrative management tools, for use by learners, teachers, and administrators. The Utility also permits networking and interaction among users. The Utility provides immediate upgrading or changes in educational programming and information bases; an exciting channel for those with good ideas about educational programming to get a hearing for their ideas; an in-place marketing and distribution system for publishers and educational software developers, while protecting against software piracy; local control of curriculum; and, in general, opportunities for learning excitement and enjoyment. The Utility system has applications in elementary and secondary schools but will have tremendous possibilities in other kinds of education settings. The Education Utility is like nothing that currently exists. Yet, it is the next logical step in the use of telecommunications and microcomputer technologies in education, able to build positive cooperative relationships among corporations, educational institutions and communities to make the information resources of the world available to everyone.

Hardware Components

In designing the architecture of the Education Utility, the developers of the hardware system attempted to adhere to a number of design objectives for the system, including:

1. The system should provide a simplified, economical, and manageable method for delivery and updating of different types of software to a classroom, such as
   a. Educational programs and applications
   b. Administrative tools and Utility software
   c. Administrative applications;
2. Teachers should have a great deal of control over the system;
3. The system must provide low cost access to the electronic information from within the classroom, such as
   a. Local data bases
   b. Remote data bases
   c. News services
   d. Information services;
4. The system must provide for a low cost inter-classroom message system;
5. The system must create an environment that would encourage software publishers to participate in the Utility through at least the following provisions:
   a. Reducing the opportunity and need for software piracy
   b. Providing a single, low-cost distribution method for vendors
   c. Paying royalties to vendors on a usage-related basis;
6. The hardware architecture should allow a school district to start with a basic classroom configuration and expand in a modular fashion, thus protecting the school's original investment.

The system developed with these objectives includes two broad components: a distribution network and an in-school network.

Distribution

The Distribution Network will provide the telecommunications facilities to transfer information resources from the national repository to the in-classroom networks. (Note: throughout the remainder of this chapter, the term *classroom* will be used to mean any educational setting that houses a Utility.) The Distribution Network will have four components:

* The *Network Control Center* (NCC) will serve as the central control and distribution point for the network. This computer facility will be the central library where all information will be stored and the main distribution point for getting that information out to the states and in-school networks. The NCC will also provide the necessary administrative controls for the Utility system, such as accounting and billing. In addition, the NCC will serve as the primary point of contact with existing data base suppliers, such as The Source, the various news networks and other kinds of data bases that users of the Utility might wish to access.

* The *National Backbone Network* will serve as the connection between the NCC and the various state computer affiliates (see below). It will transmit information from the NCC to distribution points located in each state. There are a number of possible carriers of information that will be used, including satellites, packet networks, dedicated telephone lines, dial-up 800 type telephone service, and FM or television broadcast systems, using their subcarrier or secondary audio program channels. Eventually, when the volume of use in the Utility increases substantially, it is expected that satellite transmission will be the most common carrier for the National Backbone Network.

* The *State Affiliate Computer Centers* will be franchises of NIU and will have contractual rights to market the services of the Education Utility in a prescribed geographic territory, most often a state. In some cases, a franchise may be defined as more than one state, or possibly less than an entire state. The State affiliate computer centers will eventually serve as a "central switch" or gateway for distributing information from the Network Control Center to the State Network, which in turn distributes information resources to in-school networks in each school or school district. The state computer center will provide two-way communications, transmitting information from the NCC to schools, and requests, information, etc., from schools to the NCC.

* The *State Network* connects all in-class networks within a given geographic area. Each state network will be developed using the most efficient and effective media distribution system available in a given state. Figure 1 contains an illustration of the basic elements of the distribution network of the Utility.

The flow of information to and from an individual user of the Utility might be summarized as follows: A student (or teacher) indicates an interest in using a particular educational software program in the Utility. The request would flow from the school, through the State Network, to the State Affiliate Computer Center. If the particular

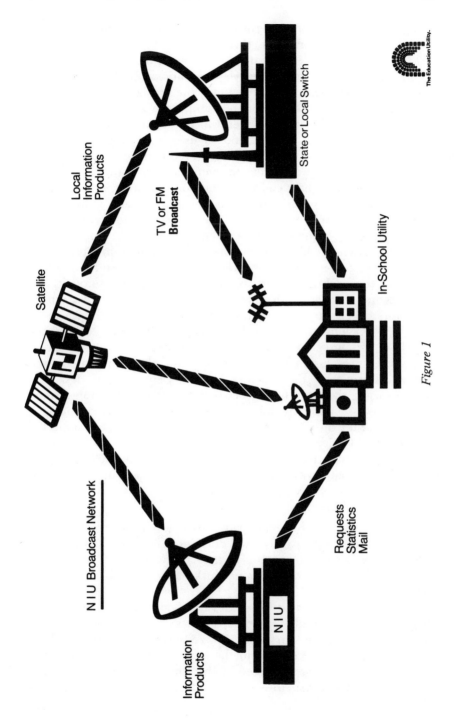

Figure 1

program is housed on a permanent basis in the State center, the program would be sent back, through the State Network, to the in-school network. If the program is not housed in the state computer center, a request would be sent via the National Backbone Network to the Network Control Center. Once the message is received, the NCC would transmit the requested program via the backbone network, to the state computer center, which in turn sends the program, via the state network, to the school or user requesting it.

All of this may sound rather complicated and time consuming. It should be noted, however, that the movement of information along these networks will happen in only one of two ways: in some cases, a user may need some information immediately, and if that information is stored only in the NCC. The request would travel through all the electronic highways outlined above, and the user would receive the information at his or her work station almost instantly. Such access is less cost-effective, however, because the transmission would occur at the peak (and most expensive) telecommunications times. The second way most information would be transmitted is during off-hours, when programs that are planned for use during a given day, week, or longer, can be ordered ahead of time and stored at the in-school computer, to be accessed by learners directly, thus saving expensive transmission costs. In either case, the information itself makes its way from the Network Control Center to the desk of a student using the same basic electronic highways. This transmission network is essentially invisible or transparent to the user, making it unnecessary for the user to be technologically sophisticated about the system. The Utility is designed so that users need not be concerned about *how* information reaches them. They can concentrate on *what* to do intellectually with the material once they have it.

The In-School Network

Within a given school, another network would be created. This network would be the part of the Education Utility that actually gives users access to the information in the Utility. Figure 2 contains an overview of the in-school. This network has several discrete components:

* The *Classroom Computer* provides in-school network control, systems management and storage capabilities for all the users in the school. This computer (an AT&T 3B2/310 or 400 in the first phase of the Utility) will receive from the state network the information and programs that are requested by the school; store those materials until needed by users; store various administrative and other tool

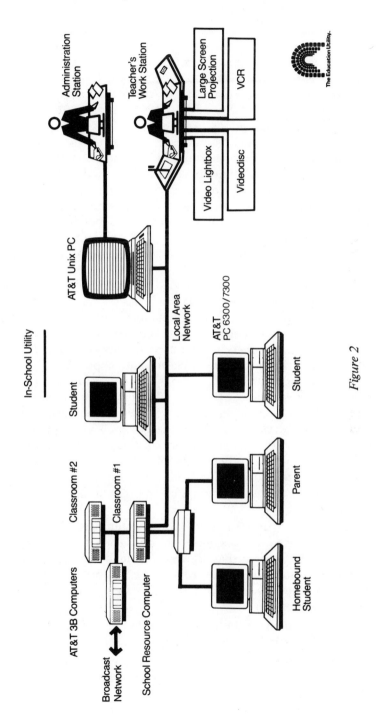

Figure 2

programs for use by teachers, administrators, and students; and store information on student characteristics and other instructional and administrative data bases generated for and by the school.

* *Work Stations* are the microcomputer terminals actually used by learners, teachers, and others to directly access the Education Utility. These terminals (AT&T's PC 6300, 6300X, and/or 7300 UNIX) will run MS/DOS applications as required by the user; permit the user to communicate with other users; and, of course, permit the user access to any of the electronic information contained in the Utility. Up to 30 microcomputers can be connected to a classroom computer; one of these microcomputers, however, must be designated as a teacher work station. The system will permit each of the 30 users to be working with different programs simultaneously or to form smaller groups of users to work on a common program. In some cases, the teacher may assign *all* students to work on a common data base or program.

* A *local area network product,* provided by AT&T, which utilizes an Ethernet transmission technique, will be used to transfer data from the classroom computer to the work stations, and vice versa. This connection will, of course, be invisible to the user. Another of AT&T's local area network products will be used to connect multiple class-rooms and all work stations to the classroom computer.

Hardware at individual work stations can be customized to meet the needs of a given school or district. Printers, for example, should be part of the configuration. In some cases, video disks may be interfaced with the Utility at the teacher work station or at some student work stations. At the teacher work station, the capacity to use cable television and other kinds of media may be added and integrated within the Utility. The Utility will permit a variety of such hardware configurations, depending on the requirements of a given educational setting.

To support this hardware system, various system software programs have been developed. For example, the in-classroom network, that part of the Utility system that allows individual users to access the Utility's information, will be controlled by a software system known as the *Network Control Program Product.* This systems software program will make it possible for:

1. Teachers to manage the flow of work to individual students and to match learner characteristics to instructional characteristics of certain programs;

2. Security systems to be established to protect data on the system, and to prevent piracy of software materials;
3. Metering of system usage for applications, student, and system functions;
4. Simplified management of user files and system administration capabilities; and
5. Access to the telecommunications facilities provided by the broadcast network.

The Network Control Program Product permits the teacher to assign an application or a specific series of applications to each student. The selected application (or program) is automatically downloaded to a particular work station. This kind of function would not be possible without the software packages that have been developed. There are numerous other such software packages that are essential to the smooth operation of the Education Utility. These packages will not be discussed in detail here, in part because, like other technical parts of the system, they are designed to be invisible to the user. What the user cares most about is that the system works. Precisely *how* it does what it does will be a little interest or concern to most users.

In addition to these hardware and software components, plans have been developed for linking home or other remote microcomputers into the local school's Education Utility. These remote hardware configurations will permit parents, for example, to dial into the school computer to inquire about grades, lesson plans, or homework; send and receive electronic mail to and from school officials; or engage in training on courses or topics being taught in the school so that the parent might be better able to help students with homework. The homebound student, using the same system, will be able to receive homework assignments downloaded into his or her home terminal, permitting the student to interact with information in the same way he or she would if physically present in the school.

These, then are the basic hardware components of the Education Utility. The system is being designed carefully to guard against technical obsolescence and to expand as an individual school district's needs for the Utility increase. There are, of course, many technical details behind this general description of the hardware components. From the user's perspective, however, the critical feature is that the hardware system is flexible, adaptable, and easy to use, not inconsequential characteristics of a system that provides so much information and power to individual users.

Information Resources in the Utility

While questions related to hardware and systems software are of interest and concern to educators, questions related to what kinds of information and/or educational resources will be available through the Utility are perhaps of even greater concern to most educators. Increasingly, educators seem frustrated by the lack of quality of educational software currently available for use on stand-alone microcomputers. Before buying into yet another educational technology, educators will want assurances that the Utility will indeed deliver a broad range of quality educational programming and other information resources.

This section contains an outline of the kinds of information and educational resources that will be in the Utility. Before presenting that outline, however, it is important to make several general points about the Utility's plans for information resources.

The Utility is designed to be an *open* system. That is, the system will accept software and information resources from many sources, as long as that software is compatible with the operating system (MS/DOS and UNIX) of the Utility. The Utility should thus serve as a stimulus for individuals and organizations to begin to design quality software, taking advantage of the computing and distribution power of the Utility system. The system should open the doors for fascinating entrepreneurial development efforts, as people with good ideas will now have a way of getting those ideas into the marketplace. Software companies can put substantial resources into materials development, knowing they will be protected against piracy. Individual users will generate unique ideas as they work with the system; these users will be encouraged to submit their ideas for distribution throughout the Utility system. The openness of the Utility will, in all likelihood, create a grassroots groundswell for quality instructional materials, motivating individuals and companies to develop quality materials.

A second point to be underscored is that the Utility is designed to be user-driven. If users need materials, information, or programs that are not currently in the system, those needs should be made known to NIU. NIU has made a commitment to find, or cause to be created, materials that users want and need. The result of this commitment is that the resource base in the Utility will be dynamic, constantly changing to reflect marketplace demands. As educators make requests, and see them honored, even more requests will follow, setting into motion a kind of dynamic development process.

Finally, it should be pointed out that, at the time this book is being written, the Utility is about to begin operation. The system will at the outset contain a relatively limited amount of information, compared to what will be in the system six months or a year from the beginning. Conferences with publishers throughout the nation currently are being held to work out agreements for the distribution of a wide variety of information, software, video and printed materials. Those with ideas already began to contact officials at NIU, even before the system was announced officially. All of these activities bode well for the future of the Utility system, but the remarks that follow about software in the system at this point must be viewed as concepts rather than as reality. There is little doubt, however, that interest among publishers and software development houses, as well as individual writers and program developers, is very high.

What follows is a preliminary inventory of the kinds of information resources that users of the Utility eventually will be able to access. As more experience in working with the Utility is gained, additional categories of information resources undoubtedly will be added to this preliminary inventory.

Learning Tools

Users will have available to them via the Utility a number of tools useful in pursuing certain learning or instructional goals. The Utility will provide, for example, word processing programs, useful to most learners in improving their writing abilities. Spreadsheet programs and other kinds of analytical tools will be available. In time, it is hoped that the Utility will provide access to numerous programming languages.

These tools certainly are available with current technology. Why should the Utility be used to obtain access to them? First, the importance of providing these programs is to enable learners to use them in conjunction with other parts of the information available through the Utility. The Utility provides means for an *integrated* system of information and analyses. Another observation is that the Utility's network control center will offer enhancements or updates in these programs. This means users will not have to buy all new software packages. There are tremendous factors of availability and cost at stake here.

Reference Sources

Various kinds of reference sources and reference search sources will be available to users of the Utility. It is anticipated, for example, that dictionaries and encyclopedias of various kinds will be included in the information system. Other common library reference books might be available on the system. In certain continuing education fields, various technical manuals might be available on the Utility.

The Utility also might include a number of indices that students can use to search for information on a given topic. In some cases, the materials referenced in these indices might also be included in the Utility system, while in other cases the indices will direct learners to use certain materials in the school or community library.

In addition, the Utility will provide access for learners to certain established search services, tailoring resources to an individual learner's information needs at a given point in time.

Lesson / Program Software

One of the most important kinds of information resources available on the Utility will be educational software developed for microcomputers and/or other kinds of computer technologies. A substantial number of software publishers already have expressed interest in and willingness to have their materials entered into the Utility system; it is expected that most software producers will want to take advantage of this ready made market for distributing software.

What is likely to happen, over the long term, is that much higher quality educational software will be developed, given the instructional power of the Utility. Developers will have greater flexibility in designing good software, and more incentive to do so.

The Utility, through a mechanism such as the Academy of Learning Technologies (see Chapter Six) could aggressively identify specific areas of need for new educational software and promote developments in those areas. Furthermore, the demonstration center network, as proposed in Chapter Six, also could stimulate creative software development.

News and current events

The Utility also will make available, probably through wire services, news and current events information that can be integrated by the teacher into instruction. The Utility will provide a "real time" window on the world for every learner. Teachers will be able to scan this material on a regular basis and decide when particular news items are germane to instruction.

Textbooks and other print materials

The Utility information system might also contain a certain number of textbooks, as well as other kinds of print materials, that are currently being used in elementary and secondary schools. Several observations should be made about this particular information resource. First: in most states, certain textbooks have been adopted, or approved, for use in the schools in a given state. In most subject areas, a number of texts are put on the approved list, from which a given school may select one or more of the texts for use. In most cases, however, teachers in a particular classroom do *not* have access to *all* the approved texts, but must work with only one of those texts. Most teachers find that a single text is often inadequate, or not quite right, for what they wish to teach. The economics of text purchase, however, make it impossible for a district to buy multiple texts for a certain class or subject area. By placing **all** approved texts into the Utility, NIU could remove this single text limitation. Teachers and learners could draw from *all* approved texts, as needed. Furthermore, teachers and learners would no longer be required to use a certain single text from cover to cover, as is now the case. A teacher could customize a textbook for a given student by selecting chapters (or even paragraphs) on a certain topic from a variety of available texts, downloading those chapters to the classroom printer, and presenting a student with a customized copy of a textbook. The possibilities are exciting indeed. There are also, however, many issues to be resolved with publishers on this point. It is not clear at this time if publishers with texts on state approved lists will agree to having their materials on the Utility.

Another significant advantage that would be realized by learners and teachers from having textbooks in the Utility system is that those textbooks can be updated regularly, adding new material as needed, and those changes would be instantly available to learners. In most districts today, once a substantial investment has been made in a textbook series, the district is both reluctant and often unable to replace those texts in a timely fashion. As a result, students often learn from outdated texts. The Utility has the potential to change that situation. In some fields of study, this updating capacity is vital. As a nation, we cannot afford to have our young people learning material that is outdated. Of course, the significance of the updating function is considerable in certain areas outside elementary and secondary education as well. The ability to provide state-of-the-art information, for example, is at the very heart of most continuing education efforts.

Textbooks (and printing more generally) brought about a major revolution in how formal education was conducted. Today, we take textbooks for granted and sometimes overlook the tremendous impact of the textbook on the curriculum. This point is discussed in more detail later in Chapter Four. The Utility could take us the next logical step beyond the instructional power of the textbook by giving learners access to many textbooks, by customizing texts, and by being able to update texts on a regular basis, in a manner that can be afforded by school districts. It is also likely that the Utility will be of great help to the teacher in more effectively integrating material from textbooks into an overall instructional strategy. For publishers, the Utility holds the promise of an in-place marketing system and the opportunity for even more learners to use the textbooks of a publisher. It is likely that certain texts will remain physically in many classrooms. In those instances, the Utility provides supplemental materials by granting access to additional texts not physically available in a given classroom. The Integrated Instructional Information Resource (See Chapter Four) will unable a teacher and a learner to most effectively use *multiple* resources.

Simulations and Games

The Utility will include in its information resource banks, a number of simulations and games designed for higher level intellectual processes. As the Utility system develops, increasingly sophisticated simulations undoubtedly will be created and made available to learners. The Utility can, for example, be used in conjunction with video to create realistic simulations of scientific experiments. Simulations will permit learners to have educational experiences that would be quite impossible if all schools had to have the specific laboratory equipment and expertise for the actual experiments.

Vocational/Career Training Materials

The Utility eventually will make available to learners a host of materials related to vocational/career preparation and counseling. For example, the Utility might provide learners with certain vocational preference assessment instruments which they will be able to use through a Utility terminal, receive feedback on the results, and then explore materials relevant to the learner's vocational interests.

Assessment Tools and Procedures

The Utility will contain an assortment of assessment tools and procedures that can be used by teachers, administrators and learners to make assessments of learning outcomes, learner characteristics, goal priorities, or any other kinds of information needed in teaching and learning activities. For example:

1. Standardized tests of various kinds could be administered through the Utility. Test security could be assured; data could be quickly scored and reported, also using the Utility.

2. Assessment information required by state boards of education could be collected, analyzed, and reported, using tools available in the Utility.

3. Teacher-made tests could be developed, using items contained in an item bank in the Utility. These tests also could be administered, scored, and reported through the Utility. More importantly, test results could be systematically integrated with other information about individual students, to help shape individualized learning programs for all students.

4. Procedures for regularly and systematically evaluating educational software could be built into the Utility system, making it possible for teachers and learners to both evaluate instructional materials and consult evaluations made by others in making decisions about what materials to use.

5. In may states, basic or minimal requirements for learner outcomes have been established. The Utility could include tools and procedures for assessing the extent to which these basic requirements are being met and to report this information as appropriate.

6. In some states, schools are required to report certain kinds of data, in the form of a "report card," to the community and the legislature. The Utility would permit the aggregation of data needed to make such a report card.

These are but a few examples of the kinds of assessment tasks that would be greatly facilitated by using assessment tools and procedures available through the Utility. Assessment is a sensitive and sometimes very controversial issue in education. Great care must be taken to protect the privacy of all learners and to assure security of the data gathered by using various assessment devices. Because the Utility is user driven, individual users, be they teachers or school districts (or other kinds of education institutions), would be able to select what they need from among the assessment tools and procedures available via the Utility. What is important is that a range of assessment tools would be available to users of the Utility.

It is also worth stressing that the Utility provides an opportunity for teachers to more effectively use assessment data to design and implement instructional strategies. Too often, assessment data is of little use to teachers because the data cannot be integrated feasibly into lesson planning for a class as a whole or for individualized educational programs. The unique character of the Utility should overcome many of these constraints.

Curriculum Alignment Procedures

The Utility also will contain a powerful instructional planning tool, developed by the Educational Products Information Exchange (EPIE), using EPIE's Integrated Instructional Information Resource, which makes possible a curriculum alignment process tied to classroom curriculum management. More will be said about this process in Chapter Four. Briefly, EPIE's curriculum alignment process enables teachers to select or develop instructional goals; identify from the Utility information resources base and other sources, materials that have been demonstrated to be directly related to teaching toward those goals; and select from a bank of assessment items or procedures those items that directly assess accomplishment of the instructional goals being pursued. Research conducted by EPIE has produced convincing results that, in many classes in the United States, goals, materials/strategies, and assessment procedures are *not* aligned properly. We are testing students on material that has not been taught. We use materials that bear only marginal relationships to the goals we are trying purportedly to achieve. The curriculum alignment process represents one very effective way to correct this situation. As will be described later, EPIE's alignment process already has been focused on some content areas, such as mathematics. Other areas are currently being developed. The curriculum alignment process is an incredible tool for curriculum planners, teachers, and learners alike, and will be a prominent aspect of the tool resources available through the Education Utility.

Prototype Lessons and Learning Plans

While the Education Utility is designed to be under the management control of teachers, who will want to adopt an individualized style in using the Utility, it might be helpful to them if model or prototype lesson plans, focused on certain concepts or topics, were available for inspection on the Utility. These plans would not be *prescriptive*, but rather suggest or illustrate lessons that could be used with the Utility as an instructional tool.

Over time, and with input from Utility users, an inventory of prototype lesson plans could be put into the Utility information resources base. Teachers could peruse these plans, organized by topic, to find good ideas about lessons used in other places. Each teacher could then modify these lesson plans to fit his or her unique instructional plans.

Similarly, the Utility resource base could contain a number of prototype *learning* plans, designed to guide an individual's learning program. These plans might be extremely valuable for teachers and learners alike as one means of stimulating creative individualized programs of study.

Classroom management plans and tools

The overriding intent of the Education Utility is to make individualized education possible for all learners. If that goal is to be accomplished, it is clear that teachers will need a great deal of assistance in managing classrooms where 30 individual students will at various times be working on 30 different projects. In recognition of this important administrative reality, the designers of the Education Utility have been at work creating classroom management plans and tools for use by teachers using the Utility. The goal is to provide a unique administrative and instructional management system that will be open to all vendors of software who wish to contribute tools to the resource base of the Utility. Many classroom management packages are on the market today, but a large number of them are tied exclusively into a particular vendor's other software programs. Because the Utility is striving for an open architecture format, classroom management packages used with the Utility will need to be compatible with a wide variety of educational software.

Classroom management tools currently being developed for the Utility's resource bank will be modular, each module performing a certain instructional or administrative management function. The modules will be usable in a "stand-alone" format, but, more importantly, also will be usable in an integrated fashion. It is this integrated capability offered by the Utility that represents an important breakthrough in day-to-day classroom management and that will make it feasible to develop individualized programs.

Among the classroom management functions for which modules may need to be developed are the following:

1. Lesson planning
2. Attendance keeping
3. Objectives/goals setting
4. Testing procedures
5. Test output analysis and reporting
6. Instructional prescriptions
7. Mastery test
8. Gradebook maintenance
9. Performance/progress reporting

The basic purpose of many of the modules developed to deal with these kinds of functions is self-evident, but it might be useful at this point to elaborate on several of these potential modules, to give the reader a better understanding of the kinds of functions each module might perform.

The *Lessons Plans* module, for example, might be a logical starting point for a teacher who wishes to construct a lesson plan that will support individualized learning for all students. The automated lesson plan program will provide a template into which the teacher can input objectives for a class, break his/her program into modules, and then into a series of lessons per module. From there, the teacher can make individual assignments for students. This module should thus permit a teacher to prepare a lesson plan for a class as he/she has done in the past but to supplement that plan with electronic lessons available through the Utility. Any redundant work that has historically been performed by the teacher should be eliminated with the electronic lessons plan module. Once the lessons plan module has been completed by the teacher, the teacher will be able to call up some of the other kinds of classroom management modules (e.g., the instructional prescription module) and develop specifications for individualized programs of study, consistent with the overall lesson plan developed earlier. By integrating other classroom management modules with the lessons plan module, the teacher will be able to track individual performance against instructional objectives and determine what actions would be best to help individual students realize their instructional goals. The lessons plan module is designed to facilitate classroom planning.

Or consider the *objectives setting* module. Those who find instructional objectives to be an effective way of organizing instruction could establish objectives and/or select topics for a class, a group, or individual students with an objectives setting module. The intent of this module is to enable a teacher to access national, state, or district objectives, or to insert his/her own instructional objectives. At the national level, there could be included in the Utility resource's bank at least one, and possibly more, sources of statements of objectives which the teacher could review and select from. Eventually, it is hoped that these objectives banks will develop standard categories of and labels for objectives and that software developers will include references to them when specifying instructional objectives for a particular software lesson. Individual states or school districts will want to insert their own objectives into these objectives banks and, perhaps, to recommend lessons, programs, and/or tests keyed to those objectives.

To facilitate a teacher's selection of instructional objectives for a particular class or student, lists of objectives germane to the topic or skill under consideration would be presented to a teacher, probably through a menu format. The teacher could indicate by pressing a specified key on his/her terminal which objectives should be included in a lesson being planned. Then the objectives setting module would present the teacher with a summarized list of objectives he or she has selected and would provide opportunity for the teacher to revise, add to, or delete any of the objectives in the summary list. A final list of objectives would then be presented to the teacher. Furthermore, the teacher should have the option of setting *priorities* among the objectives. This set of objectives can then be used as input to the next classroom management module, such as, for example, the *testing* module, where assessment items and procedures are developed to match the instructional objectives that have been selected.

The classroom management modules suggested above, and others that will be developed as the Utility matures, are clearly not meant to *replace* the functions that a teacher performs but rather to make those functions much more do-able and feasible. The modules offer resources for teachers to accomplish critical tasks in ways that have simply not been feasible before. As will be noted in Chapter Four, individualized education has long been a dream and a hope of educators but has seldom been realized, largely because of the complexities involved in managing classrooms where individualized programs are attempted. The Utility's classroom management modules should help a great deal in the logistics of managing individualized education on a large scale.

School Management Plans and Tools

In a similar vein, the Utility eventually will contain a number of modules designed to help with many of the general management tasks that must be performed by school administrators. Functions such as scheduling, budgeting and reporting are necessary and vital responsibilities of school administrators, but those tasks tend to become all-consuming, often to the exclusion of instructional leadership the administrator might wish to perform. Programs available through the Utility should help administrators carry out management functions more effectively and efficiently. Also, these programs should be developed with the recognition that the schools of tomorrow will require an integrated approach to information management. (More about this topic in Chapter Four.)

Research and Evaluation Updates

Fundamental to the development of any major social or educational intervention is a commitment to ongoing research and evaluation, as a means of expanding the knowledge base about how a phenomenon works. The designers of the Education Utility have been concerned about creating an ongoing research and evaluation capacity. Several mechanisms for accomplishing this function are currently being discussed and are outlined in Chapter Six of this book. Most notable among them is the proposed Academy of Learning Technologies, which is viewed as a focal point for research and evaluation activities related to the growth of the Education Utility.

If research on the Utility is going to have an impact on *practice*, some means must be found to disseminate research findings in ways understandable to users. One way to accomplish this goal is to provide to users, via the electronic mail and electronic bulletin board features of the Utility, a research and evaluation update service. On a regular basis, users could consult a particular data base in the Utility's information resource base to obtain research and evaluation studies that may be of interest and help in improving educational practice. These studies could be reported in a variety of forms, but one of the most compeling aspects of this service would be that the research studies reported could be linked to practice in a very conscious way. This kind of information service will stimulate both research and better use of research results.

Exemplary Practice Updates

Another kind of information available to users of the Utility might be a portfolio describing exemplary practices of the Utility. Users who have employed the Utility in creative and interesting ways may want to share their experiences with other users. Certainly, such portfolios would be a source of ideas and inspiration for anyone who has a Utility and is looking for ways to improve their instructional strategies with it.

These are some of the resources that users will find in the Utility's information resources bank, and thus available to all users of the Utility. In addition, of course, the Utility offers electronic mail service, possibilities for interfacing with other media and other kinds of services. At no time in history has this variety of information resources been available to teachers or learners, in an integrated format, and accessible at a cost that is affordable. Teaching and learning could be profoundly affected by the Education Utility. Furthermore, it is likely that the Utility will stimulate the excitement and enthusiasm of people with an untapped well of pent-up creative energy. Many people may be willing to invest their time and effort in creating educational resources of the highest and most creative quality because the Utility makes it possible to disseminate those resources broadly and because the impact on teaching and learning of those creative resources will be evident. The materials available immediately in the Utility will be but the proverbial tip of the iceberg. Who knows what could happen if the people of this nation, and of the world, decide to invest in quality education? The Utility could just open the door to that prospect. The Learning Society may be in sight.

A Scenario of the Utility at Work

It may be useful at this point to present a hypothetical scenario of how the Utility might be used in a particular educational setting. This scenario is meant to illustrate how the Utility might fit into the instructional strategies employed by a teacher or learner, assuming availability of the kinds of information resources listed above. Other scenarios certainly would be developed, but the following may help illustrate the Utility at work.

Seventh Grade: A Lesson in Social Studies

Ms. Jones has 28 students in her seventh grade, third period class. The class is slightly smaller than her other classes due to certain scheduling problems. The students represent a mixture of academic abilities and interests, as well as a socio-economic and ethnic groups. Ms. Jones has found the class as a whole to be willing to work fairly hard at times but also very much into the social developments and interactions that might be expected of seventh graders.

Ms. Jones has created a unit of instruction which attempts to help students understand the development, over time, of population centers, and something of the social, economic, political, and cultural factors that exist within groups of people in society. She has called the unit of instruction, "Why do people live where they do?" At the outset of the unit, Ms. Jones wants students to develop an understanding of some of the geographical reasons people have chosen to live where they do. She then plans to move on to explorations of the social dynamics involved in population areas and to contrast life styles in different population centers.

Ms. Jones' classroom is equipped with an Education Utility facility, with 29 student work stations, and a teacher's work station. In addition, Ms. Jones' room has a large screen projector, tied into cable television. She also has a VCR available to her.

The unit of instruction is scheduled to begin on a Monday. About a month before that day, Ms. Jones scans the Utility index to find instructional objectives that may be of relevance to what she wants to teach. A review of the data bank reveals a half-dozen objectives statements that are very much in line with what she wants to cover. Using the lessons plan module, Ms. Jones indicates which of the objectives she wants to use, then enters four additional objectives statements that describe other instructional goals she has for the unit. One keystroke brings a summarized list of objectives to Ms. Jones' monitor. After looking over the list, she decides to eliminate one of them. She erases that objective and is once again presented with a summarized list of objectives. Ms. Jones is satisfied with the list and has a copy printed.

Ms. Jones then commands her microcomputer to search the Utility information base to find electronic material that is suggested for teaching each of the instructional objectives she previously selected from the objectives bank. The system provides a listing of titles of materials germane to each objective. Ms. Jones requests a preview of some of these titles. She first is given an abstract of the materials (which, in this case, turn out to be educational software) and then an opportunity to preview any of the materials. She does look at two pieces of software, decides that one of them looks good and notes that piece of software.

In addition, Ms. Jones has her own ideas about materials that might be relevant to her unit of instruction. She calls up three textbooks from the data bank, checks the table of contents of each and decides to look in greater detail at a chapter from one of the texts. She likes what she finds and notes that chapter. She also wants to use certain data bases of population figures; she locates those data bases, checks them to be sure they contain the kinds of data she wants and notes those data bases. Finally, Ms. Jones checks the utility index for maps of various kinds, locates the ones she will want to use and makes a note.

Ms. Jones is also concerned about the assessment or testing process she will use to determine who learned what. She checks her curriculum alignment program in the Utility and locates test items that match with some of her instructional objectives. She also notes, however, that the system does not contain enough testing items; she is now aware that she will have to use the Utility's testing module to create additional items. She will do that later.

With a good sense of what instructional materials will be available to her from the Utility and with an idea of what additional resources she has physically in her classroom, Ms. Jones begins to sketch out how the instructional unit will work. Using her lessons planning module and other classroom management tools, she identifies instructional activities and timelines, as well as content to be taught and skills to be learned by the students. The unit will unfold something as follows:

1. Ms. Jones begins with a meeting of the whole class to explain what the unit is about. She hands out a list of the objectives of the unit to each class member. She also reviews with the class the kinds of projects in which the students will be engaged, and describes how the students' learning will be measured. She indicates that each student can review each objective whenever he or she wants a reminder by calling up the objectives and a brief explanation of each from the Utility.

2. The class then views portions of a video broadcast (in this case, excerpts from the Turner Broadcasting series, *Portraits of America.*) The class talks about the video, focusing on why people seem to have chosen to live where they do.

3. Ms. Jones then makes an initial assignment. Each student is to select from a list she prepared a city or town in the United States. Each student is to locate information about that town or city and to gather certain information about the city, such as population, population growth, history, etc. Each child then works from his/her terminal to locate, using appropriate indices, relevant information from the Utility's data base. Students are asked to enter the relevant data into a "shell" format, created by Ms. Jones. Once this work has been done, Ms. Jones is able to aggregate and summarize these data across all cities being reported about and to develop a nice summary sheet comparing data about each city. Those summaries are made available to each student. When appropriate, the class will meet as a whole to discuss the implications of the data.

4. Ms. Jones then asks students to read material selected from a half-dozen textbooks available in the classroom. Ms. Jones, as indicated earlier, has reviewed those texts, found some chapters from several of the texts that seem appropriate, and now assigns those chapters to all students.

5. By this time in the instructional unit (possibly a week has been spent in the unit thus far), the class has established a general understanding of what the unit is about and, substantively, the factors that seem to be important in influencing where people live. Ms. Jones decides there is enough common understanding in the class to permit individualizing instructional programs. Taking into account the learning profiles of her students (stored in the Utility system), she develops a number of individualized programs, such as the following:

A. A group of four students is asked to explore the role *rivers* have played in influencing where people live. Students use a program developed in conjunction with a recent PBS television series on great rivers. Using a videodisc player, these four students engage in an interactive program designed to show how population centers have built up around rivers. The program provides basic information for students to write a report (using a word processing program), which they are able to share with the rest of the class. To prepare the report, students are required to search out the Utility data base to find additional information relevant to their topic.

B. One advanced student takes on an assignment that requires her to develop a survey instrument and to send that instrument, via the Utility's electronic mail system, to a sample of 200 students, living in 15 different urban centers around the world. The instrument contains 20 questions which the students being polled answer by typing their responses into their own terminals. The results of the survey instrument are transmitted electronically to the student in Ms. Jones' class, who uses a statistical program in the Utility to analyze the data. The student then writes a report for the rest of the class.

C. One of the students in the class has severe reading problems. The teacher uses a program from the Utility that stresses the development of reading skills. The teacher is able to modify the general reading skills program to feature content related to the theme of the instructional unit.

D. Two students work together to create a maps project. Using resource materials available in the Utility information bank, the students construct a number of maps, with the assistance of the graphics capabilities of the Utility. The maps illustrate some key points about where people live and to offer, from a geographer's perspective, some factors that appear to influence where people live.

With the knowledge of what kinds of resource are contained in the Utility, and with information about the learning characteristics of her students, Ms. Jones is able to create other similar kinds of individualized programs of study. Thus, small groups of students, and individual learners, are pursuing topics germane to the main theme of the instructional unit and Ms. Jones' instructional objectives. Students move at different speeds, exploring different kinds of information and completing a range of projects. Ms. Jones is able to monitor the work of the students from her work station but also has ample time to move among the students while they work, making observations, suggestions, etc.

6. As the groups, and individual learners complete their independent work, Ms. Jones brings the entire class back together periodically, to examine the work of each of the students in the class. For example, the student who has conducted a survey has finished her data analysis and prepared some tables the teacher thinks will be interesting to the class. The teacher calls up those tables and has them displayed on each student's work station terminal. As the class examines the data, led by the student, the teacher is also able to point out critical findings and have the student who conducted the survey talk more about those findings.

7. At some point, the teacher administers an examination to all the students, based on the material that has been studied in common. The results of the examination are scored and reported by a testing program in the Utility. The teacher is able to determine which students seem to have learned the material as planned and which have not. For those who have not met the instructional objectives, the teacher develops individualized programs designed to help learners gain the skills or knowledge specified in the instructional objective. This may require calling upon additional information from the Utility, such as other software programs keyed directly to the objectives not being met by the students. The Utility classroom management programs permit Ms. Jones to continue to monitor and track student progress and to know when each student has met the requirements of the objective.

It turns out that the unit Ms. Jones has developed actually was created in collaboration with another teacher, in a school district nearly a thousand miles from Ms. Jones' school. The two teachers have been communicating with each other about the unit, but now it is time for the *students* in the two classes to communicate. Using the electronic mail capacity of the Utility, students are paired up between the two classes and begin to share with each other the concepts they are learning. This kind of electronic communication greatly adds to the richness of the learning experience, as the students both gain new knowledge about the topic, and learn how to communicate more effectively with people they do not personally know. The experience is highly motivating for nearly all the young people, who ask that the communication be permitted to continue beyond the time limits of the instructional unit.

8. Also using the electronic mail capacity of the Utility, several of the students in the class contact a professor in a university who has particular expertise in the area of the social dynamics of living in highly urban environments. Students send questions to the professor,

who responds by electronic mail directly to the students. The answers to the questions are, of course, extremely valuable to the students, but so, too, is the experience of learning how to use a valuable *human* resource.

9. One of the students in the class comes down with a fairly serious illness during the course of the instructional unit. The student is not allowed to physically return to school for a number of weeks. That student is able to keep up with the class, and with her own work, by connecting her computer (borrowed from the school library) with the school computer and working as though she were physically in class. When this student returns to school she is not behind in her studies because of her access to the Utility.

This is but one very brief scenario of how the Utility might be used on a day-to-day basis by a teacher in a seventh grade classroom. Other scenarios, perhaps more complex or simpler, could be created to show the Utility at work in a variety of settings and for a variety of purposes. The Utility provides a great deal of flexibility for both the teacher and the student, to both select instructional objectives that are appropriate and to pursue those objectives until they are accomplished. The teacher has vast resources to draw upon to assist students, and classroom management tools to make the whole instructional strategy work. It will take any teacher, or any learner for that matter, a certain amount of time to learn how to use the Utility creatively. Once teachers and learners become comfortable with the ins and outs of the technology, the quality of what is offered in our educational settings and institutions should be greatly enhanced and the level of personal excitement and enjoyment of learning unmatched.

Major Partners in the Education Utility

Finally, it may be helpful to the reader to know what roles each of the major partners in the Education Utility System will actually play as the Utility is implemented. Following is a brief description of the roles to be played by National Information Utilities Corporation, AT&T, and the State Affiliates, or franchise-holders. It should be noted also that other agencies, institutions, and/or associations may play key roles in the Utility system. Those other partners, making up the all-important user support system being considered for implementation, are described in Chapter Six, and so will *not* be described here.

As the Education Utility matures thousands of individuals and institutions will be participants in the system. At the outset, however, a relatively few number of entities are actively involved in developing the Utility.

National Information Utilities Corporation

NIU was formed by Jack Taub who created The Education Utility concept. The corporation has provided the major leadership in making the Utility concept a reality. NIU will work with publishers and developers to obtain information products for the Utility. NIU will make sure that these products are distributed to subscribing schools. All negotiations on royalty payments and financial arrangements with publishers will be handled by NIU. NIU also will establish pricing policies and rates with schools and consumers for the Utility's information service.

As the Education Utility becomes operational, NIU will be responsible for all matters related to leasing and distribution of information, including responding to educators' requests for additional information.

AT&T

As the world leader in communications and networking, AT&T will help NIU design the in-school network and provide the hardware and software for its implementation. AT&T is also assisting NIU with developing the Classroom Management System and the School Management System. AT&T will also provide installation and maintenance services for the system's hardware.

Affiliates

State and local school districts throughout the United States have a high degree of autonomy. Dealing with elementary and secondary school educators successfully necessitates a knowledgeable and responsive local presence. Plans are underway for NIU to set up state or regional affiliates that will be responsible for handling local sales and services. The sole business of these local corporations will be to handle/coordinate The Education Utility's most important activities: installation, training, maintenance and other customer services for the local schools.

The Education Utility is a technologically complex system but is designed to be used by individual teachers, administrators, and learners as tough the system was technologically simple. What will make the Utility work is to provide users with an information-rich environment that is easy to create. The system, as outlined above, is designed to accomplish that kind of balance.

But the presence of the Utility in the American (and world) learning system inevitably will generate concerns with/or discussion about a number of issues affecting public policies. Chapter Three contains a discussion of several of those policy issues.

PUBLIC POLICY ISSUES AND THE EDUCATION UTILITY

Whenever an educational technology is proposed for the nation's schools, certain public policy matters become apparent and of great interest to many people. The education system after all touches in some form the lives of virtually every citizen, in most fundamental ways. As a result, anything seen to influence potentially the character of the education system is subject to much scrutiny.

The Education Utility will be no exception to this. The Utility may well be one of the most significant and comprehensive technologies ever considered for the education system and thus will be subjected to intense debate and discussion, as educators, parents, and others seek to understand `how education might be influenced by this technological system. The developers of the Education Utility have been keenly aware of at least some of the public policy issues that will be raised as the Utility is introduced to and into the education system. These public policy issues include:

1. To what extent and in what ways will the Education Utility enhance or inhibit attempts to gain greater equity within the education system?
2. To what extent and in what ways will the Education Utility impact on traditional local control of education?
3. How will confidentiality of information about learners be protected in the Education Utility?
4. To what extent and in what ways will the Education Utility change the historical role of the school in the community?

There are, undoubtedly, other policy issues that will surface as more is known about the Education Utility. The developers of the Utility intend to remain very sensitive to these policy issues and, in fact, to aggressively engage in policy analyses and studies to ascertain critical issues that need understanding. This chapter represents the first of this thinking about policy issues and the Education Utility.

Equity

Those exploring the Education Utility will be sure to ask how the Education Utility will either enhance the education system capacity to achieve equity in delivering education opportunities or inhibit such efforts. Basically, will the Education Utility permit *all* kinds of learners, irrespective of economic background, race, sex, geographic location, or other such personal characteristics, to have equal access to the information and opportunities provided through the Education Utility and to have an opportunity to succeed at those opportunities? Or, the obverse of that question, will opportunities for both access and success be *denied* certain kinds of learners *because* of their economic background, location, race, sex, or other personal characteristics?

Issues related to equity are extremely complex and deeply rooted in the social and educational history of this nation. The literature on the topic of equity is massive. The evidence we do have strongly points to areas of significant inequities in both access and success within our education system. In spite of years of concentrated efforts to reduce these inequities, they remain, to a greater or lesser degree, throughout education. Some in our society have extraordinarily rich opportunities in education, while others have deplorable few and low quality options open to them. What educators, parents, and policy makers want to know is whether the introduction of the Education Utility will merely exacerbate these existing inequities or help reduce them.

In some respects, it could be argued that *most* of our citizens, young and old alike, have been discriminated against in our education system by our general inability to individualize instruction. We have yet to achieve anything near the ideal of the learning society and thus have not made available the kinds of learning opportunities to everyone that we should.

It also is the case that *some* individuals have been denied such opportunities more than others. And, frequently distinctions among who gets what from the educational system are highly correlated with economic background, race, sex, and, increasingly, age. Will the Utility make any difference in this situation?

The Education Utility is designed to promote equity in terms of access to educational opportunity. The concept of the Utility is, in one sense, aimed toward equalizing opportunities for everyone, as the *information* transmitted via the Utility is transmitted without prejudice. The poorest student and the richest student may each work on the same educational program, if they have access to the same kinds of resources. Blacks and Hispanics will access the information in the Utility with equal keystrokes of their terminals. The *information* in the Utility will not discriminate.

Furthermore, the Utility is designed to reach anywhere. Those living in the inner city will have access to the Utility, as will those in remote rural areas. In fact, the Utility will make information available to people anywhere in the world.

In concept, then, the Educational Utility represents a tremendous stride forward in making education more equitable by providing equivalent educational opportunities to all individuals.

The Practicalities

But there are *practical* aspects of all this which will determine if the concept of the Utility becomes reality. While information available on the Utility will be available to everyone in equivalent form, availability depends on having access to the Utility, by having access to terminals connected to the Utility. Once again, the potential for equity could be thwarted for it can be argued that some school districts and individuals, by virtue of their socio-economic status, location, or some other factors, may not be able to afford access to the Utility. Equity will not be served merely by having good information available to all who access the system; the key to at least a part of the equity issue lies in the economic aspects of acquiring the Education Utility.

Issues of equity can be examined from a number of perspectives, but for purposes of this chapter equity will be discussed in relation to the following questions: Who will have access to the Education Utility? Will all users be adequately prepared to use the Utility, even when access is gained? How might greater educational and social equity be fostered by the Utility?

Historically, various social benefits, including access to quality educational opportunities, have been unequally distributed among segments of our society. The rich tend to receive more than the poor, whites more than minorities, and suburban dwellers more than either rural citizens or inner-city residents. In some areas, men gain more from the benefits of society than do women. As a society, we have found countless ways of distinguishing and discriminating.

AT&T/NIU have been very aware of this critical economic factor in designing the Utility system. These corporations have made a significant commitment to assuring that people and institutions in all kinds of settings and conditions will be able to tie into the Education Utility. Details about the financing to the Education Utility are still being worked out. For purposes of this chapter, it should be pointed out that the ability to financially and technically *acquire* the Utility, in some form, is clearly pivotal to accessing the power of the material found on the Utility, and thus to achieving its social and educational goals. The economics must be solved.

Economic access clearly is one critical component in achieving equity through the Utility, but questions of equity are not answered solely by assuring that everyone has *physical* access to the Utility. Too often, this quickly becomes a revolving door: some who acquire access to education find themselves out of the system prematurely, due in part to lack of adequate preparation to function within the system, and in part to the lack of preparation of teachers and other educators to work with them. The preparation of both learners and teachers to work effectively with the Education Utility becomes central to any discussion of equity and the Education Utility. Chapter Five contains a detailed account of the training needs of teachers, administrators, learners, and parents regarding the uses of the Education Utility, together with some plans as to how those training needs can be addressed as part of the overall implementation plan for the Education Utility.

Thus, access can be thought of as more than merely claiming that certain services or information are available. If those services are not made available in a form that can be successfully adapted by different people, then availability alone may not be sufficient to claim the equity issue has been solved. In some cases, access may mean providing pre-requisite remediation for those who use the Utility so they can effectively utilize the information on the Utility. In other cases, access must include a kind of *psychological* and/or cultural access, a personal sense on the part of the learner that success can be achieved and a parallel sense on the part of teachers and administrators. The point is that a consideration of *access* may involve an investigation of the *conditions* of access, those environmental and personal factors that spell the difference between access (and thus equity) as a theoretical idea and access as a reality.

For example, there are concerns regarding "gender bias" in the use of computers or computer systems.* It may be useful to explore

---

* This section was contributed by Karen G. Brown, College of Education, Northern Illinois University.

this particular issue, this *condition* of access, in more depth as a way of illustrating the kinds of issues that surface as subsets of the broader equity issue and that must be addressed in plans to implement the Utility.

As microcomputers increasingly have become prevalent in elementary and secondary schools, a disturbing trend is being observed by classroom teachers, namely, the differential use of computers by girls and boys. The tendency of boys to be more involved in the use of computers is particularly ironic, given that some of the most prominent computer "pioneers" were women. For example, the defense department's computer language ADA is named in honor of Ada Lovelace, the world's first programmer. Also, 100 female programmers operated ENIAC, the first major computer built in the 1940s.

In spite of this early involvement of women in computers, today computers appear to be viewed as a primarily male domain. In advertising for computers, few women are shown in pictures, and when females are present, usually they are depicted in an "assisting" role.

It is particularly important to assess how computers currently are being used in education and to what extent *all* students have equal access to and instruction in the use of computers. The need for such an assessment is clearly important in the case of the Education Utility. What happens in the classroom has an important bearing on the possible career choices of students and whether or not those students will become fully participating adults in the new information age. We have here a substantial question of equity.

Gender Questions

Four important gender questions which educators need to consider regarding the education of all students, and with respect to the Education Utility, are:

1. What is the extent of the gender discrepancy?
2. Why is the gender discrepancy important?
3. What causes the gender discrepancy?
4. What can be done to counteract the gender discrepancy?

What is the extent of gender discrepancy?

Numerous studies have indicated differential use of and attitudes toward computers by boys and girls. Because many schools now require basic computer literacy as part of graduation requirements, observing only numbers of boys and girls enrolled in such basic courses may give one a distorted picture of the actual situation regarding computer use. More valid measures are obtained by looking at students' discretionary use of computers, such as before and after school use, computer clubs and computer camps, as well as electives such as advanced computer programming courses. It is in the discretionary use of computers that the greatest differences between boys and girls are detected. In a recent study by Miura and Hess (1984), a survey of 23 summer computer camp directors in the United States indicated that the ratio of boys to girls (total N = 5,533 students) enrolled in the camps was approximately three to one (74% boys to 26% girls). These researchers found that as the cost of the camp and the grade level increased, the proportion of girls enrolled decreased. The authors comment:

> Differential enrollment was even more striking when tallied by level of course offering. . . . Only 5% of those enrolled in the more advanced assembly language courses were female. (p.22)

Equally striking results were obtained in a study by Leukhardt (1981), who looked at the selection of elective courses by approximately 200 gifted high school students. While 90% of the boys chose to take a computer course, only 10% of the girls selected that option. An interesting aspect of Leukhardt's study is that her study population was comprised of gifted students only; presumably, "lack of ability" was not a factor influencing the girls' decisions.

Other studies yielding similar findings regarding differential participation by boys and girls in summer computer camp programs include studies by Lucking (1984) and Diem (1985). Lockheed and Frakt (1984) reported that in one study of 400 students taking an introductory computer course, nearly half of the boys, but no girls, used the computers at the computing center outside of the required class time.

Not only do males and females differ in their out-of-class use of computers but they also differ in their attitudes toward computers, as indicated by numerous studies (Chisholm & Krishnakumar, 1981; Collis, 1985; Lucking, 1984; and Smith & Stander, 1981). Typical results of attitude surveys indicate that girls on the average are decidedly more negative in their attitudes toward computers than are boys. Males are more interested in computers and more self-confident than females about their ability with computers (Collis, 1985).

Given that a gender discrepancy does exist with respect to computer use and attitude toward computers, it is important to ask if the discrepancy is an issue of equity, and if the Education Utility is likely to exacerbate the discrepancy?

Why is the gender discrepancy important?

The gender discrepancy in computer use and attitudes is significant in part because of the occupational and economic choices made by students. Lucking (1984) comments:

> Regardless of why certain differences exist, it seems clear that females may be eliminating themselves at a very early age from career choices by these negative attitudes. Because computers are being used so pervasively across all of business, industry, and the service sectors of our economy, females may be penalized in their career options because of these predispositions. (p. 82)

Miura and Hess (1984) indicate that the gender discrepancy in computer use and attitudes toward computers will increase inequities in the labor market because of the increasing importance of technologies utilizing computer programming skills. These researchers state:

> The new technologies may threaten gains in educational and career opportunities for women and minorities that have been achieved at great effort in the past two decades. (p. 22)

Even if a person does not intend to become a computer professional, computer literacy is necessary for everyone. Gilliland (1984) argues that in order to be a participating member of society, a person must be computer literate. She warns against a polarized society in which

> . . .only a few will exercise the power given by knowledge of technology, while the rest flounder, unprepared to make decisions on the many technical issues that will affect their lives. Unless we take strong, positive steps now, a majority of those unprepared will be women. (p.44)

Fisher (1984) reports on one teacher's graphic depiction of the importance of computer skills in the marketplace. He states:

> One high school work processing class has a sign on the door that reads:

SALARIES

SECRETARIES	$10-15,000
DATA ENTRY CLERKS	$12-18,000
PROGRAMMERS	$15-25,000
SYSTEMS ANALYSTS	$20-50,000

> The point is not lost on the students in the class; many have signed up for a programming class. (p.25)

Because there is a definite gender discrepancy in the use of computers and attitudes toward computers, and because this discrepancy is perceived to be detrimental for women, particularly in occupational and economic areas, we clearly have a case for arguing inequities exist in this domain. But why?

What causes the gender discrepancy?

One factor which may account for a considerable proportion of the sex discrepancy is the perception of computers as a "male domain." Evidence of the association of computers with males is found in a number of areas, including advertising for computers, computer software and role models such as teachers. Sanders (1985) analyzed 172 photographs in computer magazines depicting those who were directly involved with computers. Her findings confirmed that computers are indeed portrayed as a male domain. Thirty six percent of the photographs depicting passive computer use (e.g., watching others use computers) were of females. In the photographs portraying active computer use (e.g., using the computer oneself) only 17% of the pictures included females. Sanders concluded:

> Teachers and parents who read such magazines can hardly be blamed for expecting that computer users will be male. No less an authority than the Director of Educational marketing for Apple Computer, Gregory Smith, was recently quoted as saying, "The buyers of Apple computers are 98 percent male. We do not feel that women represent any great untapped audience." It is easy to see how such an attitude can become a self-fulfilling prophecy. (p.23)

Computer software also tends to perpetuate the perception of computers as a male domain. Computer software, particularly games, exhibits a style inherently more appealing to boys than to girls, e.g. emphasis on competition, aggressiveness, violent action and destruction, and loud noises. Even educational software may exhibit sex bias which favors males. Fisher (1984) states:

> While many subjects have no inherent bias (addition hardly has a gender bias!), the symbols and images used with them can carry strong sex biases. For example, one math drill program races cars across the screen to display students' scores. Another has rockets blasting off after each correct answer. In another, out of 10 stories, 8 are about boys and the remaining two are about dogs. . . . The general message comes across loud and clear-computers are for boys, and not for girls. (p. 24)

Another indication of the sex bias of computer software is offered by a study in which junior high students evaluated the titles of 75 randomly selected pieces of software for gender orientation (Lockheed & Frakt, 1984). Almost 40% of the titles were rated as being written primarily for males, while only 5% were rated as being of interest to females.

Another factor contributing to the perception of computers as a male domain is the association between computing and mathematics. Frequently, computer classes are taught by mathematics teachers, and sometimes mathematics courses are a prerequisite for computing classes. Demetrulias (1985) comments:

> ...the mathematics and science anxiety of female students as reported in the research literature may have a legacy in computers as well. (p. 133)

In addition to outside influences, parents may also consciously or unconsciously reinforce the perception of computers as a male domain. Sanders (1985) conducted a survey among seventh and eighth graders who had computers at home. When asked who (among family members) used the computer most at home, the responses indicated ". . .relatively intense computer use by males and rather diffident use by females" (p. 24). Thus, the role modeling in the home appears to portray computers as being more appropriate for males than for females. The research of Miura and Hess (1984) suggests that parents are willing to spend more money on computer camp courses for boys than for girls. Such messages are subtle but clear, i.e., computers are more appropriate for boys than for girls.

Given that there are gender differences in the use of computers and attitudes toward computers, and that these differences do have certain detrimental consequences for females, it is appropriate to inquire into what might be done to eliminate or reduce gender discrepancies, and thus at least one measure of inequity.

What can be done to counteract the gender discrepancy?

In a recent study by the American Institute for Research, Schubert, DuBois, and Wolman (1985) identified 12 circumstances and situations that impede computer access and use. The barriers include:

1. Lack of encouragement for females and minority students to use computers;
2. Potential value of computer learning more apparent to males than to females;
3. Bias against females and minority students in software and advertising;
4. Prerequisites irrelevant for computer access and instruction;
5. Limited computer access for females during free time;
6. Underrepresentation of females in computer leadership roles;
7. Dominance by one student over another during computer time;
8. Pressure from peers not to participate in computer activities;

9. Underrepresentation of females and minority students in computer clubs;
10. Inappropriate location of computers within schools;
11. Inability of teachers and students to recognize and deal with problems in computer learning; and
12. Shortage of qualified personnel for computer teaching. (p.41)

From their study, the authors developed a resource titled *Ideas for Equity in Computer Learning*. For each of the 12 barriers listed above, the authors used examples from their data base to illustrate what happens to students, given each barrier. Schubert, et al. also offer ideas for educators in appraising their situation, raising awareness of a barrier, taking action to remove or lessen the barrier, and assessing the results. For example, the action recommended in dealing with barrier number 7 (dominance of one student over another) includes: (1) the establishment of rules for working in teams; (2) the requirement of group cooperation to complete an activity; (3) the rewarding of cooperative efforts; and (4) varying team partners and group members.

Another structured program for counteracting gender discrepancy in computer use is offered by the Computer Equity Training Project, funded by the Women's Educational Equity Act Program, U.S. Department of Education (Sanders, 1985). The five general approaches recommended to encourage girls to use the computer during their free time are the following:

1. Structure the free time. A sign-up schedule that guarantees computer time for girls is important because the reason for computer equity effort in the first place is that boys usually crowd out girls in the computer room;
2. Make the herd instinct work for you. . . .target groups of girls rather than individual girls as potential computer users;
3. Foster friendliness at the computer. . . .encourage social interaction in the computer room;
4. Push the computer as a tool, not toy. . . .stress school-related computer uses such as word processing, data base programs, and graphics; and
5. Bait your hook. . . .provide girls with activities they like to do — find out what that is by asking them and by offering them choices — and they will keep coming back. (p.27)

In addition to the above programs, other suggestions are offered by Lockheed and Frakt (1984). They recommend that teachers encourage female participation by making four changes in their classroom and curricula. First, teachers can change the image of the computer room as "male turf" by reserving the room for girls at specific times. Second, teachers should eliminate software that is oriented toward one sex, including a blanket prohibition against game playing. Third, teachers can provide access to computers for students who do not have computers at home and can demonstrate uses of the computer other than game playing or programming. Finally, teachers can stress application programs in their introductory courses, rather than computer programming.

Further Steps

Although accomplishing these many suggestions would do much to counteract the sex discrepancy which now exists regarding computer use, there are additional steps which could be taken to enhance female participation. For example, a parent education program might be useful in helping them understand the ways in which they may be discouraging (perhaps unconsciously) their daughters from preparing for careers requiring computer knowledge.

Because adolescents tend to be influenced heavily by their peers, encouraging female social leaders in a class to participate in out-of-class computer activities may result in greater female involvement with computers. One way to enhance female involvement is to emphasize the variety of uses (other than games and programming) there are for computers. For example, female students could be shown how computers could be helpful to them in their extracurricular activities.

Another step that could be taken to reduce the gender discrepancy is to involve all teachers in the school in the use of computers. If the use of computers was integrated into the total curriculum, there would be less likelihood that the computer would be viewed as a male domain. For example, computer graphics programs could be utilized in the art curriculum, and word processing could be taught and used as part of the English curriculum. If students see all teachers using the computer (and not just the math teacher, who most likely is male), the students should be less likely to view computers as a male domain.

Finally, steps could be taken to make students aware of the sex biases that exist in software and in advertising, and thus encourage them to resist such influences. A class of students could conduct their own research project on "bias in advertising" by bringing into the classroom examples of computer advertisements.

How will the Education Utility deal with this very particular subset of the larger question of equity? First, it already has been stated that the training of teachers and administrators is essential to dealing with equity issues. In this case, a part of the training provided for educators must focus on issues related to gender inequities so teachers and others consciously can assure that girls are not discriminated against in the use of the Utility.

With respect to software development, care can be taken that software on the Education Utility does not systematically discriminate against female users. More specifically, AT&T/NIU, working through the proposed Academy for Learning Technologies (see Chapter Six), can solicit the development of software free of gender bias.

The Education Utility, by its design, is highly suited to address social interaction issues that appear in the literature to be of particular importance to females. Small groups and team work can be facilitated through the instructional characteristics of the Utility. Students will be encouraged to work with one another, across race and sex lines. The isolating tendencies of the stand-alone microcomputer can be eliminated by the Utility. The Utility is designed to deliver instruction in ways that are not discriminatory towards females. Here again, however, teachers and learners alike must be helped to use the Utility in ways that are *not* discriminatory.

Gender bias, as stated earlier, is but one subset of the broader concern for equity. This extended example was chosen not necessarily because gender bias is the most *important* subset of equity but merely as a way of illustrating the thinking that must be explored to reduce inequities. The Education Utility is designed to have the *potential* for gaining higher levels of equity in the education system. Furthermore, the Education Utility includes, as a major part of its implementation plan outlined in this volume, the means for all to gain access to the system, and once there, to have equal opportunities to access the same fine quality of information and materials. Even given the *potentials* for achieving greater education equity, the Education Utility must be intelligently and sensitively planned and implemented so that the capacity of the Utility to enhance equity is achieved. The goal of greater equity in education is a difficult one to achieve, but the Education Utility should provide one means of achieving it. This brief discussion merely flags the issue for more attention.

Local Control

There is another public policy issue of considerable importance: the extent to which the Education Utility will promote or impede local control over education. Any education intervention that hints of national or even state control of or influence on education at the local level evokes strong emotions.

The issue of control of education basically centers on who decides what will be taught, by whom, with what strategies and materials, and with what results. Control essentially is a question of who determines matters of curriculum and personnel in the local school. Historically, local school districts, working within parameters established by the State Board of Education and, to some extent, federal restrictions, are recognized as responsible for the nature and quality of education in their communities. This tradition is fiercely protected by local boards, in some districts more fervently than in others. Suggestions of a "national curriculum" are looked upon with great concern and opposition. The standardized testing movement alarms many, for example, because it essentially could remove curricular authority from local school boards. Even state requirements for teacher certification are viewed with suspicion by some boards. In spite of consistently strong allegiance to local control over school curricula, there is surprising homogeneity of curricula throughout the nation, due largely to the dominance of curricula by a small number of textbook publishers. No matter: what counts is that officials in each district, within some given parameters, feel they have the opportunity and authority to make curricular choices unique to that district.

Key decisions about education, made at the local level by governing boards, administrators and teachers, tend to concern what content will be taught in the classrooms, what instructional methods will be used to teach that content, what educational materials will be used in classrooms, what measures of learner outcomes will be used and how education will be financed. Within the context of these questions swirl many issues, some heatedly debated within the local community. For example, issues related to the teaching of creationism generate much debate, as do those of censorship in the school library. Programs for children with special needs often are debated, as are certain extracurricular activities. These issues can generate serious debate within a community, but any divisions often are forgotten when it is perceived that *outside* influences are impinging on the schools. Thus, while it may be difficult to arrive at a working consensus within a community with regard to certain curricular matters, it is generally the case that a consensus can be reached in a hurry, among disparate citizens in a community, if the community senses that its control over education is being compromised.

The Utility and Local Control

Given the nature of the Education Utility, it is inevitable that questions will be raised about the extent to which the Utility will support local control of education:

1. The Utility has a national control center, which contains information that will be available to users of the Utility. Will we (as a local community) be able to determine which of that information our children will and will not be able to see or use?

2. If we use the Utility, are we required to follow a certain curriculum that is determined by the developers of the Utility?

3. Will the materials we *do* want our children to learn be included in the Utility?

4. Will we be able to contribute to the Utility with materials we think are especially important?

5. Will we have any control over what individual students will be able to access from the Utility via home terminals? That is, can we monitor what our children are engaged in?

6. Can we control whom our children communicate with, via the electronic mail services of the Utility?

7. Will the materials and programs in the Utility system enable us to meet state requirements?

This list of questions probably will be expanded as more people become aware of the Education Utility. It is possible now, however, to provide some replies.

The Education Utility is designed to be "user driven." That is, the Utility becomes what the user wants it to be. The Utility represents a giant resource pool and a system for delivery of items from that pool to the user, to be used in ways judged appropriate by the user. There are really two critical operations in the Utility. The first could be portrayed in a conversation between officials of the Utility and users: "We who work the Utility have at our disposal this vast array of resources, including data bases, education programs, textbooks, films, etc. Would you, as a user, please examine our list of resources, and decide which of the things we have you would like to use? Let us know, and we will make those things available to you. *You do the selecting, according to what you want and need.*"

The second operation might be summarized: "we (of the Utility) are available to you, the user, to help locate specific kinds of materials, programs, or strategies that you would like but that are not now located in our resource bank. If you will tell us what you want, we will either find it or arrange to have it created for you, and enter it into our resource pool for your use. You may have some things that *you* have made, and would like added to the resource pool. *You define your needs for resources, and we will respond to those needs by finding or creating the resources you need."*

This message is clear: The Education Utility is designed to meet the particular resource needs of the user and to provide those resources in ways consistent with local decisions about how the resources are to be used and by whom. The Utility is designed to fit with *any* curriculum, to be useful to *any* local decisions about instructional goals, strategies, and resources. The Utility is *not* a curriculum, but a set of resources to satisfy a variety of curriculum demands. The Utility is *not* a single instructional strategy that must be used by all, but rather a set of resources that can become part of a variety of instructional strategies. The utility is *not* an externally imposed process of education, but is rather a system whereby each local community can more effectively achieve its educational goals. The Education Utility does *not* require local educators to use only what is currently available through the Utility, but offers, instead, to expand their available sources by finding and adding to the resource pool what local educators say they want.

The Education Utility is, in short, a system to enhance, rather than oppose, local decision making about education.

The Utility will contain systems permitting local educators and citizens to clarify their educational goals and to improve instructional strategies designed to accomplish those goals by accepting, rejecting, or modifying information resources. The Utility opens the doors to incredible educational resources, but local educators, through their curriculum/policy decision processes, will have the opportunity to select which resources to use in their classrooms. The Utility will help educators and learners achieve, in a richer and more effective manner, what they decide is important to pursue.

Confidentiality of Information

Another important policy issue concerns the confidentiality of information about students that may be contained on the Education Utility. The Utility will include information management programs permitting teachers to gather information about student performance and to use that information for both instructional and individual decisions. The Education Utility also could be useful for gathering and aggregating standardized test scores, permitting a variety of analyses of student performance on these tests. As an instructional aid to teachers, the Utility will permit considerable amounts of information to be gathered about each learner. Such information is, of course, vital to any attempts to individualize education. Some, however, will be concerned about what might be done with such information about students.

The issue of confidentiality of information involves at least the following questions:

1. Who will have access to student information, and how will that information be protected from those who should not have access to the information?
2. What kinds of information will parents be able to have about the performance of their children, particularly as parents are able to access the Utility from their homes?
3. How will information about student performance be reported, and to whom?
4. Will information about students be available to researchers, and what safeguards on the use of such information will the Utility have in place?
5. Who will be able to supply student information? How secure will the system be against inappropriate information?
6. In the event a family moves from one district to another, will student records be readily transferable?

While the Education Utility clearly is not the first attempt to create a computer-based information system on student performance, the Utility is the most comprehensive system yet devised. Teachers, administrators, and learners will have access to more information about learner performance than ever has existed in the past. This information will enable teachers and learners to make instructional decisions in ways not possible before, but the Utility does generate questions such as those posed above.

Developers of the Utility realize these concerns are similar to those of other systems such as the electronic transfer of funds in the banking industry. Confidentiality and security of information are of paramount concern. In the Utility system, the management systems being developed are taking into account confidentiality and security of data about students. The classroom management systems in the Utility are designed to facilitate what each user will need to know in order to do his or her job. For example:

1. What information does an individual learner need in order to accomplish a particular instructional task, and in what form does the learner need that information?

2. What kinds of information will a teacher need about an individual learner's performance and personal characteristics, in order for the teacher to help design an individualized instructional program for each learner?
3. What kinds of information will a teacher need to have about the aggregate or collective performance of a *group* of learners, and to whom must this information be reported?
4. What kinds of information about student performance must a school administrator have? How is this information best aggregated and analyzed?
5. What kinds of information will school boards and other governing boards, need about student performance, and in what form is this information most useful?
6. What kinds of information about student performance should parents have and in what form?
7. What kinds of information about student performance and characteristics will state boards of education, and other external governing boards require, and in what form?
8. What kinds of information will educational researchers and policy analysts require about student performance and characteristics, and in what form will this information be reported?
9. What kinds of information about student performance will various citizen groups demand, and what should such groups be able to acquire through the Utility?

AT&T/NIU have consulted a focus group of experts to explore these and related questions. It is evident that policies must be established to provide a clear set of directions concerning access to student information. The issue is complicated, involving finding a proper balance between protecting the confidentiality and security of information about various aspects of student performance and making important information available to appropriate parties. The issue is first and foremost a *conceptual* issue; that is, an issue of defining the parameters of the problem. Once agreement has been reached about what kinds of information, reported in what form, should be available to whom, then the practical problem of constructing the proper internal management system of the Utility can be addressed.

Major work on defining the management system of the Utility has already been undertaken, and some preliminary decisions have been made. AT&T/NIU recognize, however, that work on these problems has just begun. As more experience is gained in working with the Utility in various educational settings, it is anticipated that further refinement of the student information management system will be needed and forthcoming. Because the Utility is a user-driven system, it will be important for users to have an opportunity to work with the Utility, and then to define needs for additions to or modifications in the system for handling student performance information.

The School as Community Resource Center

Another public policy issue that may be raised by the Education Utility concerns the roles of the school in a local community. The presence of a Utility in a school very well could open prospects for the school to play dramatically different roles in the community. The school could well become a much greater community resource than currently in most communities. Following are some possible roles schools with Education Utilities could play:

1. The school might become a location for individual community residents to come (or to access the system from their homes, through telephone or cable hook-up), during non-school hours, to use the schools' Utility terminals to do a variety of activities, such as word processing, engaging in learning programs, training programs, etc. The school would need to continue functioning well beyond normal school hours for this purpose.

2. The school might become a resource *generating* unit, by selling off excess capacity of the Utility, primarily during non-school hours, to local businesses or private individuals who wish to pay for the services of the Education Utility. Some portion of the monies generated in the sale of excess capacity would revert back to the school for use by the school. This resource generating role of schools is clearly unique and may raise a number of basic policy questions.

3. Schools with the Education Utility may develop very different ties with homes in the community. The school and the home may be able to communicate in ways that have not been possible before. This communications ability may have implications of several kinds. For example, given the ability to forge new kinds of links with the home may lead the school to engage *parents* in programs of continuing education, directed both at helping parents do a better job helping their children, but also helping parents continue their learning.

4. Similarly, schools may find themselves involved to a much greater extent in providing adult education activities. Schools have always been places where certain kinds of adult learning programs have been offered. The Utility opens up entirely new opportunities in this area.

5. New kinds of partnerships between business and industry and local schools may be possible with the Utility in place. Local businesses may begin to offer services to customers, through the Utility, that have not been available in the past. For example: a local pharmacy may be able to provide for customers, on a regular basis through the Utility located in the school, updates related to new developments in pharmaceuticals of interest to local citizens. A local bank, working with school officials, may provide information about mortgage alternatives through the Utility. Or a major corporation could work to develop educational programming related to mathematics and offer that program through the school, via the Utility. The school with a Utility may well stimulate creative new ways for businesses and industries in a local area to work together to promote a community learning society and to provide training for students for locally available employment.

6. Local government officials, working through the school and the Education Utility, could engage in electronic "town hall" meetings, during which citizens could both be informed of matters of local interest and debate, and could register their feelings about these matters. The Utility and the school could thus serve as a kind of public opinion poll.

These are but a few ideas about new roles that schools (with the Education Utility) could play in a community. Once again, as more experience is gained with the Utility, new and better ideas about the school as a community resource center will be developed. But these possibilities are not without costs. For example, if the school is to truly be a community resource center, it is likely that the school building will need to remain open much longer hours and will be used by a wide variety of community groups and individuals. There are cost implications involved in being open longer. There are issues related to the "proper" relationship of an educational institution to a profit-making business. And there will be issues related to the extent to which schools should be engaged in activities that produce, rather than spend, resources. What is to be done with those resources? Will the school be seen in any way as competing with a local business? All of these issues will need to be resolved as experience with the Utility is gained.

On the positive side, the possibilities are exciting indeed. The journey called the Education Utility is toward realization of the idea of the Learning Society. What better way to move toward that kind of society than to feature the school as a major community resource center for learning and social interaction! The school ought to lead the way in promoting a community of learners, and the Utility provides a means for the school to exercise that kind of leadership. Most communities are hungry for a focal point, a way of making communities more than real estate. Communities are seeking ways to enhance the quality of life in the community: the Education Utility, and the school, provide an important means of achieving that quality of life.

The policy issues outlined in this chapter, together with others that will be articulated as the Education Utility begins to unfold, will need to be seriously addressed by both potential users of the Utility and the developers of the system. Many of these public policy issues will need to be worked out at the local level. For its part, AT&T/NIU are firmly committed to exploring these matters of public policy, for the long range success of the Utility will be determined in part by satisfactorily working through these policy issues. To that end, AT&T/NIU, possibly through the Academy of Learning Technologies (see Chapter Six), and in conjunction with state affiliates, intend to systematically will identify, study and report on policy issues which impact on the implementation of the Education Utility.

These kinds of broad public policy issues will eventually shape the parameters of the Education Utility within a community. Schools will raise other questions on how the Utility will fit into current educational forms and practices. Some of these important issues are taken up in Chapter Four.

CHAPTER FOUR

THE EDUCATION UTILITY IN THE EDUCATIONAL SYSTEM

Given the unique characteristics of the Education Utility, it is reasonable to ask how this powerful concept will fit into the existing education system. It must be seen by the nation's educators to fit, if it is to be used. It is also reasonable to ask, however, how the Education Utility might *change* education. This chapter includes a preliminary analysis of the Education Utility in the education system, with attention to:

1. What relationship will exist between the Education Utility and current school/state curricula?
2. What are the possible implications of the Education Utility for changes in instructional strategies and procedures used by teachers and learners?
3. What are the possible implications of the Education Utility for the development and use of instructional materials?
4. What are the possible implications of the Education Utility for changes in administrative/management strategies, procedures and materials used in schools?

The material in this chapter is speculative, as the Education Utility has not yet been used comprehensively in school settings. Consequently, this material perhaps is best viewed as an outline or set of guidelines, useful for the start of the journey called the Education Utility. As experience accumulates, more definitive responses to these questions will be possible. This chapter actually represents a potpourri of ideas about how the Utility might be used and with what results. The possibilities are fascinating, even at the beginning of the journey. What is most exciting is that the uses of the Utility will expand as educators and learners turn their creative minds loose with it. This chapter is thus prologue but, nonetheless, important as a starting point for the journey.

The Education Utility and Curricula*

What goes on in schools, on a day-to-day basis, is guided by the curriculum, a planned sequence of content and activities designed to produce certain learner outcomes. Each of the 16,000 independent school districts in the United States is governed by curricula, as is each of the approximately 87,000 individual schools in those school districts. By design and by law, the curricula are a function of local decisions about what schools are for and what learners are to learn. As a result, variation in curricula is considerable, although (as mentioned in Chapter Three) some research suggests a remarkable degree of homogeneity in curricula among school districts. The states have ultimate responsibility for the character of public education, including especially the curricula offered in each school district, although, again, the degree of state influence varies.

In theory, curricula could vary considerably, as each district is relatively autonomous. In fact, no school district can be truly independent. Each district operates within a complex network of state regulations, standardized tests, common textbooks and regional accreditation agencies. Funding for schools, so dependent on local community support and state underwriting, tends to depend on what extent the curricula are viewed by the public as familiar, understandable, traditional and reasonably transferable. As a result, any innovation for the public schools is closely scrutinized by a host of interested parties and special groups, including parents, taxpayers, legislators, and, of course, teachers and administrators. There will be many questions about any innovation, particularly one as potentially powerful as the Education Utility. One of the *primary* questions to be raised about a proposed innovation concerns the relationship of that innovation to the most essential of school issues: curricula. Communities want to know: Will the innovation in question permit us to

---

* Contributions to this section were made by Dr. Michael Sullivan, Assistant Superintendent for Instructional Television, Maryland Instructional Television.

offer the curricula we wish or must offer, in the way we want to offer them?

The Education Utility, as suggested in Chapter Three, is designed expressly to respond affirmatively to this basic question. Because local teachers and administrators will be able to select from the vast inventory of the Education Utility only those resources desired at the local level, the Education Utility in no way will dictate *what* must be taught in a given district, school, or classroom, nor *how* content ought to be taught. The Utility places control of the system in the hands of the user. In fact, the Education Utility *enhances* local determination of curriculum matters, through at least the following ways:

1. Eventually, the Utility will contain it its resource base the objectives or goals for each state mandated curriculum area, which will then be available to individual teachers and/or districts to reference as needed. In addition, local districts will be able to develop statements of goals or objectives, put those goals into the system and have those curriculum goals available to teachers as needed.

2. State or locally adopted texts and other materials could, over time, become a part of the resource base of the Utility. Local districts or teachers then would not be restricted to using only one, or several, of the state or locally approved materials, but rather, through the Utility, have access as needed to *all* of the approved texts included in the system. In addition, of course, other texts may be available as well.

3. Any required state or local testing instruments could be made available through the Utility, providing a more effective means of giving and recording test results as required by local and/ or state curricula and of integrating testing programs into the broader instructional program.

These are only three examples of how the Utility could assist local districts in achieving their own curricular goals. Because the Education Utility is user driven, it clearly can accommodate any curriculum pattern established by a state or local district. Furthermore, the Utility can accommodate the curriculum goals of the teacher and learners in any classroom, because the Utility contains a resource base and an access system that can be molded to fit virtually any curriculum requirements. To be sure, the *comprehensiveness* of the resources on the Education Utility will be limited when the Utility begins. But over time, the resources available through the Utility will expand to the point that *most* curricular needs will be satisfied.

In sum: the Education Utility, by its very design, will be able to support virtually every traditional curriculum and, indeed, will permit individual teachers, local districts, and entire states to continue to control their curricula, perhaps more effectively than before.

But the story of the relationship of the Education Utility to school curricula doesn't stop there.

In the current public debate about American education, there is concern about the quality of present school curricula. Increasingly, educators and other thoughtful citizens are recognizing the fundamental nature of some of the societal changes occurring. For the emerging Information Age, some see development of higher level thinking skills, encouragement of creative thinking and new definitions of personal and professional excellence as indispensable. There are concerns that the current domination of school curricula by textbooks, scope and sequence curricula, and multiple-choice tests may not be conducive to preparing young people for the emerging society. Some argue that there must be a new system which not only addresses these emerging needs but reflects new intellectual and social tools. The rate of change we are seeing in society makes it increasingly difficult to justify curricula that seems not to change, or change too slowly. Learners in the future will need to cope with situations very different from those we now experience, as in *America, Part Two*.

In light of these concerns, it is important to point out that the Education Utility, indeed, can support traditional curricula but also will be instrumental in encouraging educators to consider substantially different kinds of curricula, geared to changes in learners and in society. The characteristics of the Utility make it possible to devise curricula heretofore impossible to imagine within the limitations of our access to resources and strategies. The Utility can break us out of the historically linear approach we have taken in designing curricula. It enables us to consider curricula that genuinely provides individually tailored educational experiences. And the Utility may make it possible for us to involve learners intellectually as never before.

In some respects, the Education Utility comforts two kinds of people: those who worry that external forces are impinging on the ability of local school districts and individual teachers to determine what shall be taught, and how; and those concerned that some means must be found to devise curricula more appropriate for the future. The Education Utility can be a passive innovation with regard to curriculum, because it simply can enhance the capacity of a local site to continue to offer a traditional curriculum. At the same time, the

Education Utility can be an aggressive innovation, putting into the hands of a local community a tool capable of responding to the most creative ideas about forward-looking curricula. The critical factor is that the Education Utility's power is in the hands of the users, to be shaped in ways thought appropriate for each situation. It is, of course, to be hoped that the Education Utility will not bring greater rigidity to the curricula, although that potential exists. Rather, it is hoped that the Education Utility will inspire open and honest analyses of what is needed for the future, and that local communities will exercise the kind of curricular wisdom important to their future.

The Education Utility and Instructional Strategies*

The curriculum followed in an elementary or secondary school, or in other educational settings, provides broad parameters for instruction. Within these parameters, *instructional strategies* must be selected by both teacher and learner, to accomplish the goals set forth in the curriculum. A crude distinction is that curriculum defines the *what* and *why* of teaching and learning; instructional strategies define *how* what is to be learned will be taught.

The Education Utility has tremendous implications for the *how* of education, that is, for instructional strategies available to teachers and learners. Imagine a classroom where a group of Colorado sixth grade students, working on a project on acid rain, communicate via computer with New York students working on a similar project. Picture an after school teleconference involving teachers from four different schools in three different states focusing on teaching dyslexic children. Envision a high school teacher sending immediate feedback to one of her students completing an algebra assignment at a home terminal.

Scenarios like these can become realities with the Education Utility. A seemingly unlimited stream of ideas for innovative classroom practices is generated whenever two or more educators begin to discuss the powers of such a system.

For many, however, this enthusiasm is tempered by healthy skepticism. Experienced educators have seen innovative teaching methods and media come and go, with many failing to live up to even our most modest expectations, often despite substantial financial investments. In the final analysis, the value of the Utility to the schools ultimately will rest not with its developers, venders, or software

---

* This section was contributed by Dr. Carol Carrier, Assistant Dean, College of Education, University of Minnesota, Minneapolis.

producers, but rather with those who manage the day-to-day experiences of students: classroom teachers.

This section focuses on those day-to-day activities created by teachers to help students learn, and how the Utility will enhance them. We need to ask:

1. What is an instructional strategy? What are common strategies used in our classrooms?
2. Will teachers need to modify their planning processes to use the Utility effectively?
3. How might the Utility facilitate the use of different instructional methods, such as individualized or small group instruction?
4. What new or improved instructional strategies will be available with the introduction of the Utility into the classroom?

Definitions of Instructional Strategies

Learning occurs in the classroom intentionally and incidentally. Children learn incidentally through conversations, by observing other's behavior, by having quiet time to themselves. Intentional learning results from those activities and sequences which a teacher plans and then implements. The term "instructional strategy" will be used here to describe a planned sequence of activities designed to move the learner toward competence in mastering new knowledge or skills. Strategies represent the teacher's vision of how best to help students meet performance objectives. Strategies have three major attributes: (1) they focus on one or more instructional events; (2) they make use of one or more methods; and (3) they incorporate one or more media.

Instructional events. An instructional strategy has as its focus one or more of these nine events (Gagne & Briggs, 1979):

1. Gaining the learner's attention. Causing the learner to focus on the task and the content related to the task;
2. Informing the learner of the objective of the task. Helping the learner form expectations about why he/she is engaging in this particular learning event;
3. Stimulating recall of prerequisite information. Refreshing memory for other concepts, principles, or knowledge that relate to what is to be learned;
4. Presenting the important content. Introducing new content through various means (print, visuals, auditory, etc.);
5. Providing learning guidance. Providing instructional support, such as prompts, reinforcement or highlighting;
6. Eliciting performance. Presenting practice or application opportunities;

7. Receiving feedback. Providing learners with information about the quality of their practice;
8. Assessing performance. Requiring that learners demonstrate their competence in the new material without assistance from the instructor; and
9. Enhancing retention and transfer. Broadening the content for new learning.

Methods. How each of these instructional events operates within the learning sequence depends on the methods used. Familiar methods include the use of questions to test comprehension or of a diagram to help students understand a relationship of two or more principles. Within a typical instructional sequence, many different methods are used to ensure that these nine events occur.

Media. This term indicates how the methods described above are delivered. Textbooks, computers, films, videotapes, self-instructional booklets and worksheets are examples of media which carry methods. Any given medium can convey a variety of methods. For example, computers can use questions to test student understanding or animation to present a new concept. Textbooks can weave in analogies to guide learning or present exercises for student practice.

The most common methods and media used in instructional settings include:

Methods	Media
Questions	Textbooks
Examples	Worksheets
Analogies	Assignments/homework
Discussion	Tests
Probing responses	Films
Exercises	Filmstrips
Problems	Learning stations
Prose	Computers
Pictures/illustrations	Lectures
Gaming	Handouts
Cooperative tasks	Small groups
	Large groups
	Videotapes/disks
	Cassettes
	TV/radio
	Publications

One of the most powerful characteristics of the Education Utility, of course, is that it is an integrated technology system, capable of providing to teachers and learners alike virtually *all* of both the methods and the media listed above, in ways never possible before.

Careful attention to the selection and integration of these three components (events, methods, media) will increase the probability that an instructional strategy succeeds. To implement instructional strategies through the Utility will require careful planning because the sheer abundance of options available to the teacher will be greater than ever before.

Teacher Planning

Before examining specific ways in which the Utility might affect instructional strategies, we should consider how the Utility relates to typical teacher planning. Research has shown that actual teacher planning behaviors are much less systematic than those prescribed by traditional curriculum and instructional planning models presented in pre- and inservice training (Dunkin & Biddle, 1974). Teachers typically do not start with objectives, then generate alternative strategies, and then design assessments. Instead, teachers often begin with activities. A teacher planning a lesson on the four basic food groups may first retrieve a worksheet she developed several years ago and then build an instructional sequence around it. Like physicians who routinely prescribe the same drugs for a variety of illnesses, teachers return again and again to a limited set of learning activities.

The use of the Utility for instruction may provide a paradox. Although such a system may free up a teacher's time to perform other tasks, at least an equivalent amount of time must be invested in planning strategies which effectively use the features of the Utility. Planning time may correlate directly with the quality of the strategy. When a teacher fails to review a textbook chapter in advance, or to prepare adequate homework assignments, she/he may discover that despite good intentions, the lesson goes poorly.

Because the Utility is a new tool for teachers, they will need to ask themselves several important questions in the planning process, including:

1. **What uses of the Utility will help me achieve my objectives?** The teacher may, of course, use the Utility to establish objectives. An obvious benefit of the Utility is that it provides teachers and learners access to a greater variety of instructional materials than ever before. Computer courseware will include drill and practice, tutorials, simulations, data bases and problem solving programs. Other materials, including textbooks, films, videotapes and slides will be available. But the knowledge that these materials exist, and in such magnitude, may be overwhelming to many teachers. How will they make choices?

The Utility will give teachers substantive descriptions of the content and format of a resource along with an analysis of how well it works with students of various ages and ability levels. Decisions about which materials to use should be made only after a teacher has reviewed the possibilities. The curriculum alignment process (explained in more detail in the next section of this chapter) may be especially useful in this regard.

With respect to software, producers sometimes overpromise what their products will deliver. A publisher's brief description may imply that a program will teach new concepts when, in reality, it only delivers drills. The critical reviews or evaluations from the Utility will provide information, such as: What prior knowledge must the student have in order to use these materials effectively? Is the introduction adequate or will I need to supply one? Are practice opportunities included? Is there a range of difficulty such that students at many levels can use the material?

In addition, the Utility will allow teachers to communicate directly with one another and with colleagues in colleges and universities, across the building or across the country, about their overall reactions to particular programs as well as the best ways to use certain materials. Teachers also will be able to easily preview materials.

For teachers who wish to generate their own instructional materials, the Utility will provide several tools. Word processing, materials generation packages, and authoring systems, together with the Integrated Instructional Information Resource package, will be available.

2. **How will the Utility help me diagnose and manage student activities?** Monitoring student progress is a complex task and becomes increasingly so if different students work on different materials at the same time. The Utility will contain a management system to help teachers monitor student progress. For example, teachers will be able to select objectives from an item bank or enter their own objectives in the system. Prescriptions for instructional strategies to support the learning of selected objectives will be available. Test items to assess mastery objectives will be available on the system, or teachers may enter their own items. Each student may pursue unique objectives, as well as those shared with his/her classmates. Teachers will be able to request progress reports on individual students or a summary report of group data. Evaluation data on student learning will be available much more quickly than is presently the case. The Education Utility thus represents a genuine opportunity to individualize instruction.

3. **Will the Utility change my role in delivering instruction?** For years, the role of the teacher as a manager of the classroom has been emphasized (Joyce & Weil, 1980). The Utility will promote this management role. If the system can diagnose successfully student needs, prescribe materials or experiences and assess progress toward objectives in most subject matter areas, the teacher will be able to spend more time with individual students, in planning and improving his or her own skills.

Special training certainly will be required for teachers if they are to make the most of the Utility in their classrooms. Teachers will continue to play important role models. They will become even more instrumental in ensuring that developmental needs of students are met along with academic needs. (More will be said about teacher training in the next chapter.)

What are the implications of the Utility for teacher planning patterns? Will the planning patterns mesh with the demands of the system? It is clear that a major impact of the Utility is its potential to provide access to extensive amounts of instructional and informational material, far exceeding what can be housed in the traditional curriculum resource center, media center or individual classroom. But teachers must become familiar with these materials. Thus, the system must provide a convenient method to help teachers locate and review available materials.

Teachers will need assistance in becoming more systematic and thorough with their planning. The Utility will require that materials be downloaded into the classroom computer in time to be used within an instructional sequence. The management functions built into the system should provide this help by matching materials to objectives. Most teachers will find it important to review the quality of the prescribed materials to ensure they fit the needs of the student.

The Education Utility: New Hope for Individualized Instruction

Delivering tailor-made instruction to students with different needs has long been a dream of many educators. "Individualized instruction" was the label given to that goal in the 1960s. The term has been defined in many different ways. Here, it means an instructional strategy which is responsive, or takes into account particular characteristics of learners, and which allows for optimum learning by each student.

Unfortunately, the dream to individualize instruction has not been realized in the past. Although not insensitive to the needs of individual students, many teachers have given up on attempts to individualize instruction. Why? In what ways might the Utility alleviate some of these problems associated with individualized instruction?

A major cause is lack of capacity. There are too many students per teacher and too little assistance. For a typical elementary teacher, planning individual curricula for 25 to 35 students for 180 school days is an overwhelming task. Teachers simply do not have the time or resources to mount anything but modest efforts in this area. We know students learn at different rates, have varying needs for structure or learn from different methods, but few have been able to implement a system to accommodate individual needs effectively, especially in regular classes. One major solution to large numbers is a management system that diagnosis, prescribes and assesses students in most subject matter areas. The system must allow for the entry of teacher-made, standardized and commercially produced assessments such as those found in textbook series. The files in the system must have the capacity to be updated continuously so the teacher can obtain the current status of each individual student, in each subject matter area, instantly.

Another cause is the lack of materials or of access to them. Recognizing that a student needs visual support for an abstract concept, a teacher may be unable to locate the right approach to the content in the materials available in the classroom or curriculum materials center. The Utility, however, offers entre' to a larger bank of materials than possible in any single school district. Further, teachers will be able to use parts of existing materials, such as a page from a textbook, a segment of a videotape, or one piece of information from a database. They will be able to review materials with their classroom computer or at home terminals. A user friendly indexing system is being designed for teachers to tell them what is available in the Utility and to obtain materials quickly.

Another reason individualized instruction has failed is that it often is equated with self-instruction or isolated instruction. Some educators believe the emphasis on students working alone is an unhealthy by-product of the technology revolution. In a manuscript on cooperative learning and computer-assisted instruction, Johnson and Johnson (1985) write:

> How students interact with each other is a neglected aspect of computer-assisted instruction. Much training time is devoted to helping teachers arrange appropriate interactions between students and (a) the computer and (b) other curriculum materials, and some time is spent on how teachers should interact with students, but how students should interact with each other while working with a computer is relatively ignored. It should not be (p. 3)

The authors cite six major limitations of individualized learning by computers. They claim that such learning promotes social isolation, denies opportunities for learners to summarize orally and explain what they are learning, prevents social modeling, is not as powerful a reinforcer as peers, provides less powerful and complex feedback than is possible from peers and goes against students natural preferences for working cooperatively at the computer.

Johnson and Johnson's research, conducted primarily with K-12 students, has shown that cooperative learning activities at the computer can be more beneficial to achievement than individualized activities (Johnson, Johnson, & Stanne, 1985a: 1985b). Jeter and Chauvin (1982) suggest that the best approach to individualizing instruction is to meet the needs of individuals within a group through a balance between activities appropriate for members of the particular group and those meeting the goals of the teacher. (Note the similarity of these observations to the discussion of gender discrepancy in Chapter Three.)

While the Utility will provide a sophisticated tool to deliver self-instruction, it will not favor one style of grouping over another. Once again, the need for careful planning by the teacher is underscored. To make reasonable decisions about which groupings to use and when, the teacher will need to consider the many options available. The critical point is that the Education Utility, by its design, will *not* restrict the teacher's (or the learner's) use of a *variety* of instructional approaches. The Utility will not lock a teacher into a single way of instruction.

Another reason individualized instruction has been lackluster is much broader than the lack of teacher time or access to materials. Not knowing about student differences nor how to accommodate them are major stumbling blocks to individualized instruction. No amount of accessible material will make up for a failure to understand what is needed by different types of students. The only consistently accommodated individual difference is that of rate of learning. Consequently, self pacing of instruction often has been equated with individualized instruction.

Fortunately, some of the most interesting research in education over the last 15 years has focused on understanding how learner characteristics interact with instructional methods and media (Cronbach & Snow, 1977; Tobias, 1981). Will the Utility help with research on these basic questions about student differences? One exciting potential of the Utility is its capacity to collect student performance data from many schools all across the country. Educational research often is criticized for its lack of external validity. Findings from a study with a small sample in one geographic location may be challenged because schools demographics differ so widely. But the Utility could produce more externally valid research through data collection from many different settings. As a quick illustration, it would be possible for the Utility to look at achievement data related to time-on-task data from hundreds of classrooms. To the extent that better research will enhance the *practice* of individualization, the Utility should be valuable in promoting better practice.

In general, the Education Utility offers a long-awaited prospect for developing individualized instruction. Even before extensive experience is gained with the Utility, it is possible to imagine some kinds of instructional strategies that will be possible because of the Utility. For example:

The Student Profile. An electronic database might be constructed for each student. It would provide teachers with an instant but rich profile of important characteristics of each student. The database would be designed by the teacher and is likely to include progress on different components of the student's curriculum; learning or cognitive style; information and special problems identified by the teacher, e.g., unusual test anxiety or difficulty in working as part of a group.

The teacher could call up a student profile as needed. He/she might wish to determine, for example, if Student A needs remedial help on some aspect of the instructional unit, or the learning style information could determine if the teacher should locate special materials to help a handicapped student. Each teacher easily could update this profile.

Testing. Students could be tested at different times conveniently and with few security problems. Some students may be ready to be tested on a unit of material ahead of others. The management system could generate alternate forms of tests so that no two students will have exactly the same test form. If a student is ill but does not wish to miss a critical test, he could take the test on his home terminal. The management system would allow the teacher to check on who has completed a given test and the range of scores. Built in packages could provide information about the quality of items and the overall reliability of teacher-made tests.

Homework. Teachers could load assignments and related materials into the classroom computer and ask students to call up these materials on their home or library terminals for homework. Immediate evaluation feedback for some types of assignments would be available to learners and teachers. Teachers might establish hotlines on which students might communicate with each other about homework assignments, lessening some of the isolation of most homework assignments today.

Team Teaching. The Utility offers interesting possibilities for expansion of team teaching. The Utility could become an important "member" of a teaching team by managing information. Team members might find joint planning easier because lesson ideas are entered into the system on a teacher's terminal and sent to a team member's terminal for immediate review and reaction outside of the regular classroom day. Team members could be located in different buildings — or even in different states.

Projects. Teachers assign projects to encourage application, analysis and synthesis of information. A "problem centered" approach assumes the solving of a problem will provide a context in which information is used or discarded according to certain criteria.

The Utility could promote the use of projects as a learning strategy. Students could draw upon a much greater variety of sources of information. Current information would be more readily available because of electronic mail. Contact with experts would be easier because of the communications capabilities. Extended hours of access to materials and databases would be possible with home terminals.

An exciting outcome of introducing any new instructional technology into the schools is that many surprises are generated by teachers and students. The potential of the Utility to affect radically the classroom is much greater than for any previous technology because it will integrate many individual methods with media. There is no question that the Utility could open up incredible new opportunities for teachers. One of its nice features is that teachers could begin by using the Utility to enhance how they *currently* teach, while at the same time could learn new instructional strategies not available before. Another side benefit that is almost sure to occur: those teachers who have experienced burnout or disillusionment with teaching, will find in the Utility an opportunity for significant personal and professional renewal.

Instructional Materials*

Instructional strategies, those planned sequences of activities designed to help learners master new knowledge or skills, involve the use of varying kinds of materials. The Utility is a pipeline for the flow of information (including instructional materials) to teachers and learn-

* This section was contributed by Ken Komoski, President, Educational Products Information Exchange (EPIE) Institute.

ers. Consequently, the Utility will be judged to a great extent on the quality of its materials. To adequately address issues related to instructional materials, one must deal first with a number of hardware/software issues. These general issues will be taken up next, followed by a discussion of the current state of educational software. The section concludes with an analysis of how the Utility might influence future software developments and how software might be more effectively integrated into broader instructional strategies.

Hardware / Software Issues

School children are being taught that they live in the Information Age. And yet, although every information technology contributing to this new "age," from the phonograph to telecommunications, has been heralded as having great educational potential, the actual impact of these technologies on day-to-day educational practice has never lived up to their billing.

This is not to say that each of these technologies hasn't attracted its share of enthusiastic advocates and users — clearly the case with computers today. But, historically, the enthusiasm for each newly-available information technology has failed to mature into broad-based professional commitment and dependable budgetary support on the part of teachers and administrators. The professional commitment of all but the most die-hard enthusiasts has waned as soon as it became clear that the sort of software needed to realize a given technology's full impact on educational practice was failing to materialize. And budgetary support for the waning technology often eroded because of the need to support the next technology coming down the road.

This well-established pattern has resulted in unfortunate budgetary and pedagogical competition among individual technologies that has diminished rather than enhanced the aggregate impact of Information Age-technologies on educational practice. This competition also has reinforced a build-in reticence toward the use of these newer, software-thin Information Age-technologies by those whose loyalties lie with education's traditional software-rich technology, the book.

The most regrettable outcome of this competition among technologies, and between them and the traditional textbook, is that it has resulted in less than the best instruction for learners. Learners and teachers alike lack the technological and pedagogical integration needed to bring instructional integrity to their school curriculum. Given the number of Information Age-technologies that has entered education over the years, this lack of technological and pedagogical integration makes the management of instruction increasingly complex for classroom teachers and school administrators. Each technology has its own unique hardware and software requirements, and most of the newer computer and video technologies are evolving so swiftly that no school can sustain a "state of the art" effort for very long without taxing an already strained budget. Yet, at the present time, the budgetary, pedagogical and managerial complexities resulting from ever increasing purchases of nonintegrateable, incompatible hardware — without enough quality software and teachers trained to make effective use of that software — are not being addressed effectively by most local and state education agencies.

The reasons for the current failure to achieve effective technological, pedagogical and managerial integration of all instructional resources are many and varied. The most important among the reasons is a lack of agreement and cooperation within the education industry on the issue of technical standards that would make for greater compatibility. However, to say that a lack of cooperation within the education industry is responsible for the present lack of compatibility across so much of the hardware and software in schools is one thing; to do something about changing this reality is quite another.

This reality is, of course, the result of marketplace competition. But unlike a healthy market competitiveness that can result in better products and prices for consumers, the current competitiveness, especially among computer companies, is causing educational practitioners and educational software publishers to pay a price neither can afford. This price is destined to increase until the current technological incompatibility is no longer an issue, and the integration of all types of learning resources can be achieved with the ease that teachers and students deserve. This increased price will be paid in the form of more incompatible products, the continuation of an unhealthy commercial climate and further fragmentation of the educational market, resulting in the lack of use of the new technologies by schools and smaller profits for educational publishers.

At present, educators and the educational industry that serves them are faced with three options:

(1) Let the new Information Age-technologies continue their current incompatibility and pay the increasing price of that incompatibility;

(2) Encourage the cumbersome approach to "compatibility" currently going on in educational computing through the emulation (more or less) of one computer by another, and pay a somewhat reduced price for this reduction in incompatibility

(an option reminiscent of the story about the old talking dog: "Be pleased that he talks at all, and don't expect him to do it very well"); or

(3) Commit to a statesman-like course of technological problem-solving and cooperation dedicated to producing agreements on intra-technology compatibility and inter-technology communicability that would not eliminate marketplace competition but make it healthier.

To achieve intra-technology compatibility, competing companies within a technology type (e.g., computers) would have to follow the recent leadership of the 19 companies that currently manufacture computer interfaces for musical instruments. After a good deal of hard work, and open give-and-take, these competing companies unanimously agreed to use a standard set of technical specifications for their hardware.

Another such effort toward intra-technology compatibility is the recent work on television standards by the Advanced TV Systems Committee. It is composed of the representatives of the U.S. Department of State to the committee of the International Telecommunications Union of the United Nations. This group is responsible for setting technical standards for telecommunications among all U.N. member nations. After much opposition, a proposal, which stipulates a new global standard for high-definition television of 1125 scan-lines, was approved at the final session of a U.N. meeting in Geneva in the fall, 1985. These are highly significant developments; similar kinds of agreements are needed in other information and communication areas. The Utility, not incidentally, could be a stimulus for such agreements.

To achieve the much more technologically-difficult *inter*-technology *communicability* and compatibility, competing companies across different technology types (e.g., film and video, print, and telecommunications) would have to welcome conversion and "cross walking" from one technology to another. This is happening now in a rather simple manner across the film and video media through the conversion of films to video tapes. The major educational benefit to be achieved by such inter-technology communicability and compatibility would be that schools would be able to provide teachers and students access to any available educational software, whether computer, video/audio, or print with maximum ease and flexibility and minimum difficulty and expense, over multi-technology delivery systems. Such compatibility might inspire the development of computer, video/audio or print software that lives up to the potential of each technology and that extends the capabilities of each. One can see the obvious benefits in this for Utility users.

What ought to be abundantly clear to anyone who has reflected on the needs of educational consumers is that a primary one is for the hardware of educational technology to be essentially a *nonissue*. That is to say, the only aspect of educational technology that a potential user of that technology should have to be concerned with is the *software* he or she is going to use and how appropriate it is for his or her teaching/learning needs at a given moment. This is the idea of "transparency" of technology that was mentioned in Chapter Two.

To understand the importance of hardware being a *nonissue*, consider the following: how many teachers, learners and parents of learners concern themselves with the "hardware aspects" of education's most common technology product — the book? Yet, the common textbook contains a series of paper-thin, two-sided, information-storing rectangles that are similar in purpose (although not in shape or in means of storage) to computer and video disks. Each series of these pedagogically-related information-storing rectangles is appropriately arranged and indexed within a *hardcover* device, the spine of which enables the user to access the stored information by manipulating — with the touch of a finger — the double-sided, paper-thin storage rectangles, each of which is conveniently hinged to the spine. By doing this, and by either scanning or carefully attending to the information on these paper-thin storage rectangles at his or her own individual pace, the user may access and use for his or her own purposes the "information system" that one or more experts on a particular subject have organized by means of this time-tested teaching technology.

The reason that textbook purchasers do not think of the cover and spine of the book as its "hardware," nor concern themselves with the quality, durability and compatibility of that "hardware" by constantly comparing the covers and spines of competing products, is that such hardware has long been a nonissue in textbook technology. And the reason it became a nonissue is because all textbook publishers have agreed to produce their products to meet industrywide technical standards for hardcover book production. This was not always the case, but over time, and as a result of demands on the part of educational purchasers, these agreements were reached. Today, all textbook producers meet this common set of production and performance "hardware" specifications. One hopes it will not take as long for the producers of the newer educational hardware to reach much-needed agreement on computer and video hardware standards.

Hardware becoming a nonissue is a necessary, although not a sufficient, requirement for the effective integration of educational technology into education. The still-unfulfilled goal — even for the well-established technology of the textbook — is the creation of learning experiences that are of the highest pedagogical quality and organized to engage a learner's interest and capabilities over time. Needless to say, the "software" side of textbooks still leaves much to be desired in this regard. Part of the time, money and energy currently devoted to hardware purchasing needs to be transferred to delivering higher quality *software*.

The Current State of Educational Software: One Perspective

At this point it is reasonable to ask, "Does today's educational computer, video/audio and print software need that much pedagogical improvement?" Unfortunately, not only is the answer "yes" to all three types of software, but the *reason* for saying "yes" to all three is somewhat different for each one. It may be useful to examine each of these basic types of educational software, beginning with today's microcomputer software.

Quantitatively, the microcomputer software field is unprecedented in the educational publishing field. Never have so many products been produced in such a short span of years by so many publishers, and with no let up in sight. Yet despite what one may read in various widely-read educational computer magazines to the effect that the quality of computer software available to schools has improved dramatically in recent years, more objective research and evaluation points out that this simply is not the case.

Robert Haven of the EPIE Institute, which monitors information and reviews all known commercially-available software, reported in April 1985 on overall trends in the quality of software developed from 1980 through early 1985. EPIE tabulated software product ratings based on approximately 3,000 software reviews from 31 professional review sources. These review citations included some 700 of EPIE's own, indepth software evaluations, widely considered by educators to be more rigorous than the other sources whose reviews are cited on the database. Haven (1985) found:

(1) Rather than reaching increasing levels of excellence, overall software quality improved through 1982 but then leveled off on a plateau best described as "barely adequate" quality. While a modest number of excellent products are available, they are exceptions to the rule.

(2) Rather than taking advantage of the unique, powerful capabilities of today's computer hardware to implement new, more effective pedagogy, most commercial software efforts are mired in time-worn approaches rooted in the limitations of older media.

(3) Despite the fact that there are 7,700-plus educational software titles on the market and about 200 or more are being added to EPIE's database every month, less than half of what would be desirable is available, and most are far below the quality needed.

In Haven's words, "The educational software field, although having great potential for improving education,. . . has a lot of growing to do." (p. 2) His conclusion that 7,700+ titles do not ensure something for everyone, compares with the estimate of Braun (1981) about the amount of topic overlap in the currently available educational programs.

For example over 50 programs are devoted to the topic of "single-digit addition." It is reasonable to estimate that such topic overlap reduces the number of unique topics addressed by educational software to 1,900, only about 40 percent of the K-12 curriculum. For a glimmer of what's missing in that other 60 percent of the curricula, consider that elementary science topics — anything that students might learn about science in grades 1-4, such as seasons, animals, body systems, earth's surface, plants, electricity, — have a total of only 31 software titles in the EPIE database. Thus, Haven has concluded that the dearth of products for elementary science is one of the most serious shortcomings to be observed in the educational software field today.

But even writing off 60 percent of the curriculum, one might expect that the topics that *do* get software attention take advantage of the unique capabilities of the computer and broaden a teacher's options in meeting students individual learning needs. The truth is less encouraging.

Software can be plotted along a continuum according to the degree of structure imposed by a program and the relative amount of control it allows the user (see figure 3). Tutorial software, for example, is highly structured, attempting to "embody the entire instructional process," and allows little user control. At the other end of the continuum, computational tool software, such as a word processing program, imposes very little structure and allows maximum user control.

To many forward-looking educators, high structure/low user control software, represents a poor use of expensive hardware resources

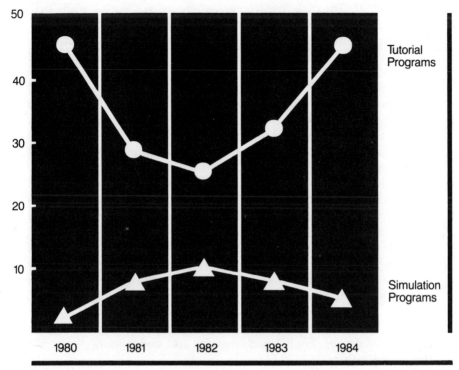

Tutorial
Programs

Simulation
Programs

PERCENTAGE OF ALL SOFTWARE BY SELECTED PROGRAM TYPES 1980–84

Figure 3

(see figure 4). Tutorials are seen as automated textbooks, while drill and practice programs are characterized as electronic workbooks. However, the present preponderance and proliferation of high structure/low learner control software is a pattern that is apt to continue for sometime.

By computing the percentage of each program type (by structure) produced in each year from 1980 through 1984, it is possible to project that the proportion of programs with drill and practice, game, data retrieval, and computational tool components will hold steady at their past and present rates. This may mean an increase in tutorial programs and a decrease in interactive simulation programs. For those educators who had hopes that educational computing would take advantage of learning methodologies that offer an alternative to traditional print-based media, a continuing increase in tutorial programs and a decrease in simulations is bad news.

These trends in software production may help explain why quality, in terms of review ratings, appears to have leveled off. Because software reviewers tend to award their highest ratings in subject areas where programs typically allow the most user control — fine arts, teaching about computers and logic and problem solving — those subject areas where programs allow the least user control — library skills, social studies, English and language arts, and reading — receive the lowest ratings.

EPIE's conclusions that the overall quality of educational software reached a plateau in 1982, "which would best be described as barely adequate," is based on analysis of two types of review ratings in the database: EPIE and non-EPIE evaluations. EPIE evaluations fall into four categories representing numerical ratings: "highly recommended" (8-10), "recommended with reservations" (6-7), "not recommended but may meet some needs" (4-5), and "do not consider" (1-3). In total, 3,101 ratings of 1,474 programs were analyzed by EPIE and other review sources. The average rating assigned by EPIE was a possible 4-out-of-10, "not recommended but may meet some needs"; the average rating of non-EPIE review sources was 6-out-of-10, a number somewhat higher than midpoint between neutral and positive. Haven consolidated the EPIE and non-EPIE ratings to conclude that the overall quality of educational software has stalled out at the lower end of EPIE's "recommended with reservations" ratings range.

Although these findings are based on an analysis of information collected early in 1985, there is no indication that educational software brought to market during the remainder of 1985 has done much to

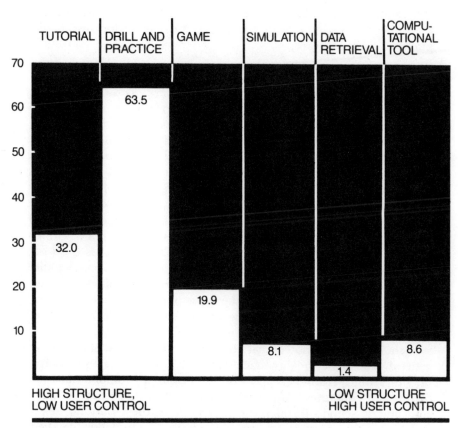

PERCENTAGE OF ALL PROGRAMS BY DEGREE OF STRUCTURE

Figure 4

warrant any major change in the basic conclusions. Unfortunately, the software situation is even worse when it comes to noncommercial, public domain software.

The Utility and the Future of Software Development and Distribution

Given the current state of educational software, as outlined above, there would be little to gain, either educationally or monitarily, by opening the Utility's electronic distribution system indiscriminately to all extant educational software. Clearly, efforts should be concentrated on distributing only the very best of the software products now on the market, which probably number between 400-800 microcomputer software programs. In addition, the Utility may want to make available to schools some of the current educational computer software developed for use on computers that are more powerful than most of the microcomputers now being used by schools. Unlike most microcomputer programs, such software usually has been designed to cover a substantial portion of the school's curriculum. Because the Utility's ability to deliver computer software is not restricted by the capabilities of the most popular school/home microcomputers, the Utility has the option to distribute the best of current mainframe and minicomputer software to its users.

It should also be noted that the quality of business software, in general, is of higher quality than educational software. This software, ranging from spreadsheets and word processing to computer-assisted design and computer-assisted management programs, can be made accessible to schools through the Utility. Thus, the Utility can select and provide the very best of today's software to students and their teachers. Once trained to use these unique Information Age resources, students and teachers will be able to get a first-hand feel for the kind of research that, until recently, could be conducted by only the most talented experts in a discipline.

Also, it is important to recognize that the Utility will be in an excellent position to foster the development of educational databases needed to develop "expert teaching systems" of the sort currently emerging from research on artificial intelligence. These could bring together the best knowledge and skills of a particular discipline to create a learning environment that has only been available in the past when exceptionally fortunate students had access to the very best textbook, the very best teachers providing individual attention and the very best reference library on a particular subject. Today, however, with the aid of expert interactive databases, it is increasingly possible to put students in direct, interactive contact with the most complete sources of knowledge available in the discipline they are studying. The traditional, "definitive" textbook in a particular discipline pales before the power of such emerging expert systems. The Education Utility is in a unique position to make such systems available electronically to a wide range of educational users — not the least of which are teachers needing to sharpen and update their expertise in changing subject areas, such as biology, chemistry and physics.

The Utility may be able to create an electronic environment through which the most expert teachers in the country may work together to create expert systems and other types of outstanding educational software and databases. Such brokering could enable the Utility to make a major contribution to the development of the quality educational software sorely needed if computers are to live up to their enormous educational potential.

Accessibility to all types of teaching and learning resources is the promise the Education Utility brings to the shaping of Information Age-technologies. Realization of this promise will depend on whether those who produce and provide teachers and learners with educational hardware and software are capable of the statesmanship, cooperation and vision needed to raise our technological and educational sights above and beyond current limits.

Because the Education Utility is as an open information system, it eventually can distribute all the basic types of educational software: computer software; video/audio software; and print materials. In addition, the Utility will adapt to all foreseeable technological and pedagogical developments. This ongoing evolution of the Education Utility relies on the new common language of the Information Age, *digital communication.* By encoding all words, pictures (motion and still), as well as all other symbols and sounds, into a compatible digital format, the Utility will deliver all educational resources to teachers and learners in a form heretofore technologically separate. Once carried to the user, the digital information can be decoded automatically. The decoded digital messages will reveal computer software, video images, audio messages and/or printed text, depending on the medium of origin. The prospects are exciting indeed.

One way of achieving this goal is for software producers to agree on a set of development and productivity standards virtually guaranteeing that educational publishers will use state-of-the-art production in whatever electronic medium they choose to produce their products. An incentive for those producers who agree to state-of-the-art standards would be access to a no-cost-to-the-publisher electronic distribution system requiring no packaging, marketing or shipping. In addition, payment would be guaranteed to the producer every time a student used a particular piece of software. This guaranteed payment-on-use would be accompanied by another guarantee to publishers: no user would be able to make an illegal copy of software used on the Utility.

These advantages should be so compelling that responsible software publishers will want to join the Education Utility's effort to provide schools with access to the highest quality software currently available. Other producer incentives could include the capability to "beta test" their products electronically in classrooms, using a voluntary network of Utility-using schools. In addition to the classroom-testing of software, the Utility's ability to gather a variety of consumer information electronically should help publishers find out much of what they need to know to make effective and timely product decisions. Such joint efforts will enable the Utility to guarantee to schools that the software developed by producers cooperating with the Utility adhere to high standards of development, testing and market research.

Another Information Age-technology that has yet to live up to its potential as an educational medium is video-audio technology. Because its origins were as a broadcast medium, most video-audio technology for education has been highly centralized, in much the way educational computing was centralized by mainframe distribution systems before microcomputer technology. The drawbacks of centralized distribution techniques were (1) a lack of flexibility to deliver a particular piece of software when needed and to deliver it directly to individual students as needed; (2) a very slow evolution toward the development of high quality software; and (3) an equally slow response to the updating of software. The result has been relatively low use of even high quality educational television programming.

Recent developments in video cassette technology (the "microcomputer" of the video industry) are bringing long-needed flexibility of distribution to educational video programming. This is leading to a burgeoning new educational video cassette industry for both school and home markets. However, this proliferation seems to parallel the pattern of mediocre microcomputer program production described earlier. A review of a representative sampling of these new educational video cassettes for *The New York Times Fall (1985) Education Supplement* by the EPIE Institute found that the poorest of the educational video products are retreads of dated animated films, labeled "classics," with a superficial "educational" overlay of superimposed visuals. And although a smaller percentage were excellent examples of high-interest, outstanding educational video software, EPIE's conclusion was that many of these products were so hurriedly produced that, in some cases, accompanying print materials were uncoordinated with the video they were supposed to support.

In response to this competitive pattern of pushing products onto the market too quickly, the Utility could provide those producing the best video products with a flexible electronic distribution mechanism with the benefits of a centralized system and without the traditional drawbacks. Additional benefits would include a capability to distribute product updates at no cost to the producer, thereby avoiding the problem of teaching with outdated materials; and the capability to electronically gather feedback on the product's use and acceptance by school and home users.

One aspect of educational video software that must not be overlooked is the increasing interrelatedness of video and computer technology, referred to earlier as "inter-technology communicability." This currently is laying the groundwork for what promises to become expert systems of almost unimaginable effectiveness, flexibility and currency.

But, as exciting and as important as computer software, video software, and expert computer/video systems are and will become, the textbook will continue to be a dominant teaching technology in the emerging Information Age. What then will be the role of the Utility with relation to textbooks? Will textbooks be electronically distributed to schools and printed on-site via high-speed laser printers? Quite possibly, although at present both economics and tradition prohibit widespread adoption of such an innovation. At the very least, it is important to consider how the Utility might make it possible for teachers and students to make the most appropriate use of the textbook.

One reason why the textbook is *not* likely to be entirely replaced in the foreseeable future is because, in so many classrooms, in so many schools, and in the minds of so many administrators and teachers, the textbook is the central, stabilizing element of the school curriculum. In fact, in many more schools that anyone would care to admit, the textbook *is* the curriculum.

This was not planned nor is it the result of a conspiracy on the part of textbook publishers. In most cases, the textbook has become the *de facto* curriculum by default resulting from a need by administrators and teachers to structure what goes on in classrooms from day-to-day, week-to-week and month-to-month throughout the school year. The textbook provides a pedagogical and managerial security blanket. It gives everyone a convenient sense of where students are and where they are going as they proceed through the curriculum.

But it also can become a crutch in the classroom and a misused management tool.

In fact, the textbook is used for so many things that it can't possibly do all of them well. Still, it is a remarkably durable educational instrument, or to be more precise, an institution. And because of its importance in educational practice, whenever education comes under fire, as is currently the case, so, too, does the textbook. Despite this current and historical criticism, however, textbooks have and will endure and, one hopes, be improved as a result of that criticism.

To understand how the Education Utility might contribute to the improvement of teaching and learning while the textbook is — and will likely remain — a given, consider the unique and crucially important role the Utility can fill in helping educators integrate technological, pedagogical and managerial functions.

Education in — and for — the Information Age means learning in an integrated manner. It means not expecting a single technology — the textbook or any other technology — to provide a pre-programmed, pre-digested approach to the integration of what is to be learned. It means learning through multiple ways that enable learners "to get it together." Most importantly, it means helping learners *and their teachers* to recognize that in the constantly changing world of the Information Age knowledge is constantly *in formation* rather than available as static, packaged *information*.

As more school administrators, teachers, and parents come to understand the need for integration of information resources, the textbook will come to be viewed differently. For instance, the textbook still may be central to the curriculum, but it may deal increasingly with more *stable* knowledge within a discipline: unchanging principles, laws, rules and invariable applications. The teaching of changing and evolving applications will be handled more effectively by the newer, more dynamic interactive computer and video technologies. Or, they also may be handled by a teacher who keeps electronically in-touch with the latest strategies for applying textbook-based principles to new situations. These strategies could be supplied by a panel of expert teaching consultants (retained perhaps by the textbook publishers) to help teachers extend their current knowledge and skills. Thus, the Education Utility may play an important role in redefining the place and function of the traditional textbook in information-rich schools by "taking over" some instructional tasks for which textbooks are not well suited.

Having said this, it is important to recognize that in many ways, today's textbooks still symbolize the undeniable educational achievements of our educational system. For a century and a half, the textbook was the instrument that made mass education of Americans economically and pedagogically feasible. But the America of mass-produced, standardized products epitomized by the textbook has been rapidly evolving into a society with options and services responding to *individual* needs and requirements. This evolution has been underway in many parts of our society for many years. However, education is among the last institutions to respond.

The Education Utility thus can make a major contribution to the inevitable shift from the standardized textbook to more individualized teaching methods, strategies and media. A key is high quality software which the Utility should promote.

The educational options the Utility opens up for teachers and learners both in schools and in homes will, of course, depend on the range of software educational publishers will produce and distribute over the Utility's "electronic highway." These software options (especially the newer computer/video/audio products) can and should create in-school and at-home learning environments that will prepare individuals to live competently and confidently in the Information Age. A pattern of achieving and exploring, exploring and achieving, will vary from one learner to the next. And the pattern also will change over time for each individual learner. To identify and match options to individual learners needs and keep track of each learner's progress will present problems for teachers and administrators that can only be managed efficiently and effectively with electronically-accessible information. Considering the textbook's still-central role in the school curriculum, it will also be necessary for a teacher to be able to select software that specifically will reinforce, complement or extend particular aspects of the curriculum covered or not covered by the textbook.

One of the many information resources available to schools using the Utility, the Integrated Instructional Information Resource recently developed by EPIE Institute (referred to in Chapter Two), will enable teachers, administrators and eventually even parents and students to identify specific software most appropriate for helping a particular learner to achieve a specific learning outcome or curriculum learning objective, or simply to explore a new interest.

In addition, this information resource also may be used by a school to discover the degree to which specific textbooks, computerized video software and tests are aligned to that school's curriculum. Being able to use information supplied by the Utility to critically assess the appropriateness of specific units, chapters and even pages in textbooks and other instructional resources can *give every school district in the nation the opportunity to make its curriculum goals the driving force behind*

the day-to-day work of its teachers and students. In this way the Utility
will help return curriculum control to local school districts.

Today, teachers constantly are being told they must become managers of information and student learning. This is easy to say to
teachers but hard for them to fulfill when most of the information
they deal with, create and use involves paperwork that most teacher
have neither the time nor the inclination to do. But in the increasingly
information-rich environment of students, helping them to grow and
to learn means helping teachers and students to manage information.
Inevitably, then, to be a teacher in the Information Age will mean
being both a capable manager of information and a teacher of
information management to one's students.

School administrators who expect teachers to be responsible for
complex information management tasks — in addition to all the other
responsibilities they currently have — must, themselves, be responsible for seeing to it that teachers have the information tools *and the
training* to enable them to integrate technology in their classrooms.
Knowing that the Education Utility, quite literally, is being designed
to function as a master information management tool for administrators and teachers should help school administrators decide to use
the Utility to move their teachers and schools into the Information
Age. The next section of this chapter discusses management issues
in greater detail.

The Education Utility and Educational Administration and Management*

To become a state of the art enterprise, the field of educational
administration must develop comprehensive and integrated computer-
based information systems to better coordinate and improve educational management. Indications of this need are found in the school
reform movement and the accompanying criticisms of education. The
expansion of educational functions into alternative/nontraditional

---

* This section was contributed by Frederick P. Frank (Professor of Educational
Administration), Muriel E. Mackett (Associate Dean and Associate Professor of
Educational Administration), Peter Abrams (Professor of Research and Evaluation),
and Jeri Nowakowski (Assistant Professor of Educational Administration), College of
Education, Northern Illinois University, DeKalb, Illinois. The comprehensive and
integrated computer-based information systems for educational management referred
to in this section are being developed by this team of professors as part of their work
with school districts in Illinois. Implications for administrator training are described
in Chapter 5 of this volume, in the section on "Preparing Educational Administrators."

settings, including non-school settings, and the related need to explore and develop alternative education delivery systems also speak to this need.

Stemming in large part from the school reform movement, educational administrators are being challenged by increasing demands to manage student achievement and staff performance more effectively while maintaining fiscal stability of the educational system.

This necessitates substantial information collection and analysis. Presently, information to meet these needs often is gathered "by hand" and maintained in cumbersome, non-integrated systems. Educational administrators typically make decisions based on information which is incomplete and calendar-driven and which may not have been collected to inform the decision at hand. In order for educational processes to be managed more efficiently and effectively, educational administrators need more comprehensive, reliable and timely information. Comprehensive and integrated computer-based information systems can provide for and manage the requisite information and are, in short, the precursors to meaningful educational accountability and concomitant educational quality.

These new, comprehensive and integrated information systems for educational management must include at least the following basic elements:

- Student Management
- Personnel Management
- Instructional Management
- Fiscal Management
- Organizational Management
- Information Management

Further, comprehensive and integrated information systems for educational management must use computer languages which are compatible. They also must have the capability to aggregate information across different populations and across many organizational levels (for example, classroom, grade, building, district, region, and state) and to interface advanced conceptualizations of information systems with advanced computer technologies.

The main premise of this section is that the technology of the Education Utility, together with the technology of state of the art microcomputers, have the potential to assist in development of information systems for educational management which meet these criteria. The chief benefit for educational administration and management of the application of these technologies will be to aid development of integrated information systems more quickly and at less cost than heretofore possible. And certainly, the kinds of educational services to be offered by the Utility require corresponding information management.

In addition, an important possible by-product of the application of microcomputer and Utility technologies could be the development of updated and easily accessible state and national data bases for educational decision-making. These data bases could aid types of research on education which virtually have been impossible in the past. A shared, national data base holds promise for enriching the educational environment for students, bringing greater control to the governance of education at all levels as appropriate and promoting educational understanding and equity among various student populations.

This section will describe the conditions which support the need for development of computer-based information systems from the perspective of educational administration and management. Included are:

- A review of past practices related to information systems for educational management;
- A description of current practices in this area;
- A view of the future, including comments on needed areas of development for microcomputer and Education Utility technologies to realize their potential for helping to improve educational management; and
- A closer look at computer-based information systems in the school setting, including a review of expanded options for administrative practice related to computer access and networks, inquiry and analysis and excellence and accountability

Past Practices

Information which traditionally was used to support administration and management of schools does not meet today's needs or emerging standards for comprehensive and integrated information systems for educational management. Prior to the use of mainframe computers in education, the limited information systems which did exist in schools were done "by hand" and focused on financial accounting and basic student control data. These "by hand" systems led to the creation of an artificial dichotomy between information needed for purposes of classroom/instructional management and information needed for typical school management functions. Because the costs of gathering and processing such "by hand" information were so great, a more inclusive information system was not considered feasible.

Limits in the available technology and related gaps in our abilities to think about or conceptualize an integrated information system also have been major contributing factors.

When mainframe computing capability appeared in education, new conceptual and technical potentials became feasible. From the outset, however, conceptualizations of new information systems did not change to match new technological capabilities. The information which was entered into mainframe information systems largely was the same kind of calendar-driven, non-integrated information that had been part of the old "by hand" systems.

As mainframe capabilities evolved, administrative thinking about information systems for educational management continued to be limited by the applications of computing to the old "by hand" systems mentality. These limits were a product of both very high costs of developing and putting in place a more comprehensive mainframe system and lack of attention by educational leaders to creating such a system. Because of the high cost of mainframe computers and software programs, administrative applications of mainframe technologies, when they occurred, tended to be implemented in wealthier school districts. As a result, the potential benefits of even these limited systems tended to accrue to those wealthier districts, further exacerbating disparities between wealthy and poor districts.

For the most part, however, even the mainframe has not influenced the nature of educational information systems. The past practices of cumbersome, "by hand" systems which do not integrate student, personnel, instructional, fiscal and organizational data continue in most school districts and other educational settings. All of these so-called past practices continue to influence information systems for educational management today, and with similar problems and outcomes.

Current Practices

The state of the art in mainframe computing in education has not changed substantially in recent years. Many have come to believe that major improvements in educational management practices have not and are not likely to be achieved using mainframe-based information systems. This is due to the fact that, following the business model, mainframe-based education information systems are continuing to develop almost entirely as separate, single purpose systems (for scheduling, busing, attendance, and financial accounting, for example). Mainframe educational software programs, while frequently very sophisticated in and of themselves, are neither comprehensive nor integrated, either across similar purpose programs or across different purpose programs. Mainframe systems have perpetuated the dichotomy between instructional management (which they tend not to include) and other management functions (which they tend to treat as central, separate foci).

Also, these single purpose systems are accessible only at comparatively high cost. They often are available only as pre-designed packages that are neither easily nor inexpensively modified to meet local needs. Very few adaptations of the business mainframe information system model have been made for the field of education, and it is questionable whether mainframe systems will prove to be more useful in the future. There is growing evidence that development and implementation of comprehensive, integrated information systems in education will be facilitated to a greater extent by microcomputer technology.

With the advent of the microcomputer, interest in and attention to mainframe capability has diminished in favor of exploration of low cost microcomputer-based information systems for educational management. Improvements in educational management practices and increases in useful information bases appear to be possible with microcomputer-based information systems. Although microcomputer technology has advanced substantially, applications of these systems need to be developed more fully within education before their potential can be realized.

In educational management, use of the microcomputer has followed the same line as its mainframe predecessor, that is, tracking those traditional financial accounting and student control data which were part of the early "by hand" systems. Software development for microcomputers, while more inventive in its applications, to date largely has followed this line of thinking as well.

The growing and fairly widespread acceptance of microcomputers for administrative work is due primarily to the fact that micros are less expensive and easier to use than the mainframe. The tendency to use the microcomputer to monitor the same data as mainframe systems persists, however, and inhibits the development of systems which are more comprehensive and integrated. The state of the art of current practice is essentially one of fairly narrow, fragmented, single-purpose systems which continue to be dichotomous with respect to instructional management and other management functions.

But there is some evidence that the state of the art is changing. In recent years, a number of educational leaders and researchers who are interested in information systems have begun to develop new kinds of microcomputer based information systems for educational management. These systems are far more broadly based than the old "by hand" systems and have begun to offer the possibility of comprehensive and fully integrated information systems for administrative/management use. It is becoming increasingly clear within the field of educational administration that the dichotomy separating classroom and instructional management from financial accounting, student control, and other management functions is indeed artificial and can and should be replaced by fully integrated information systems for educational management.

The state of the art is changing due, in part, to a fundamental equipment revolution — hardware and software — which is changing definitions of information systems and expanding the opportunity to achieve fully integrated information systems for educational management. The revolution is centered about the development of the technical capabilities of microcomputers as sufficiently powerful stand-alone systems and their capability for networking with other micros and mainframes on a scale not imagined prior to this time. Educational administrators also are becoming aware of the potential accessibility of vast data banks through a system such as the Utility, as well as the exploding developments in user-oriented software.

The future of comprehensive, integrated information systems for educational management already is being carved out of the application of microcomputer technology and related software in the educational setting. While we cannot predict all future possibilities and developments, a view of the future can be put forward at this time.

A View of the Future

This view of the future assumes that the full potential of the current equipment revolution will be realized, including solutions to any hardware, software, and other technical problems which may be encountered, either in microcomputers as stand-alone and networking systems or in the technology of the Utility itself. A second key assumption is that the greatest advantage of the Education Utility is its potential to provide a context within which educational leaders rethink their assumptions about information systems for educational management.

Integrated information systems will tend to be developed as adjunctive to the Utility, using microcomputer stand-alone power in combination with Utility networking capability. The Education Utility should have the potential to make information system software and information bases available at a cost which will allow every educational organization to participate in the coming revolution in information systems for educational management.

This revolution will be driven, not by the current prevailing business model, but by the unique responsibilities of educational managers for accountability for the education programs under their control. Emerging technologies and maturing conceptions of educational management will produce comprehensive and integrated computer-based information systems, and these will drive the evolution from current single-purpose systems to more comprehensive and integrated systems. The most dramatic change in these information systems will be the inclusion of data about many more aspects of the student experience than has been possible in the past.

The new information systems for educational management will include all the elements identified at the beginning of this section:

- Student Management
- Personnel Management
- Instructional Management
- Fiscal Management
- Organizational Management
- Information Management

The first five of these elements are fairly standard in the literature and in practice. Due to continuing inadequacies in information systems for educational management, however, these five elements have been treated to a very great extent as separate and distinct and have been built around comparatively limited data bases.

Student management includes areas such as managing student performance and progress, recordkeeping and scheduling. *Personnel management* includes areas such as personnel selection, development and evaluation and inservice training. *Instructional management* includes areas such as management of teaching and learning processes and instructional and curricular materials, as well as curriculum and program development and evaluation. *Fiscal management* includes areas such as accounting, budgeting and resource allocation. *Organizational management* includes areas such as reporting, decision making, planning and accountability.

The sixth element, *information management*, is far less standard in the educational management literature and in practice. *Information management* includes the knowledge, skills and procedures for establishing, maintaining, developing, accessing, analyzing and utilizing information which cuts across the first five information system elements. Microcomputer technology is the driving force which makes information management feasible. Similarly, it is information management which makes it possible to integrate the first five elements into a comprehensive system.

It is extremely important to note that past information systems for educational management have dealt with only some parts of some of these elements. Virtually no system has dealt with all parts of all the elements or with the whole. The capability to treat all these elements as a more comprehensive, integrated whole — built on both better and more complete data in each element and the capability to tie data together across all the elements — is the essence of the revolution in information systems for educational management.

The new comprehensive microcomputer-based information systems for educational management now being developed are characterized by the following:

- Greater orientation to management of student experience and expanded visions of what that experience might be;
- More comprehensive treatment of all six information systems elements and greater integration within each system element and across all elements;
- Extensive networking and uploading and downloading of pertinent information and extensive use of flexible, interactive microcomputer software; and
- Use of software which allows greater flexibility to meet local needs.

Quite obviously, for these systems to function well, appropriate hardware and software must be available, appropriate information bases must be available and accessible and essential training for users must be provided.

Interfaces between the new information systems and the Education Utility should facilitate both improvements in educational management and greater equality in educational opportunity. Development of these new information systems also will produce at least the following effects:

- Changes in role expectations and training needs for administrators and other professional educators;
- Increased data based educational management practices, including data based interventions in educational processes;
- Proliferation of alternative educational delivery systems; and
- Emergence of new public policy issues pertaining to educational goals, educational practice and educational outcomes.

These effects will require the careful attention of educational leaders for years to come. The whole prospect of development of new information systems for educational management also suggests the need for a closer look at information systems and educational administrators, particularly in the school setting. Information management is, in the most fundamental sense, central to increased educational effectiveness. Advanced technologies associated with microcomputers and the Education Utility are central to improved information management.

New Information Systems in the School Setting

Information management particularly is challenging in educational administration and uniquely so in the school setting. Administrators are responsible for multiple systems — achievement, personnel management, finance, transportation, health, food services, curriculum and so forth. Each of these systems must function at and across multiple levels — pre-school, primary, intermediate, junior high and high school. Within a single school district, any number of schools, unique in composition and size and each with its own problems, must be monitored and guided by district personnel. While educational achievement is a primary goal of each school, an infinite number of challenges, opportunities and constraints greet their resident educational managers.

In a very real sense, building principals bear the most responsibility for achievement and welfare of each student within their schools. They also are responsible for such diverse areas as staff effectiveness and staff development, scheduling, curriculum, school and community interactions and the school grounds. Educational management probably involves more contingencies and at the same time offers fewer mechanisms for control than management of any other type of institution.

To be able to effectively plan, monitor, direct and evaluate, the educational manager at the building or district level must rely on information. Ideally, that information is timely, comprehensive, trustworthy and integrated in some sensible fashion. Information is the single most important resource educational administrators have at their disposal to identify potential problems, dispel unfounded worries, guide decision making and manage and reward educational quality. It is precisely because information is so important to the educational manager that the technologies of microcomputers and the Education Utility provide such promising options for administrative practice. These options are most apparent in three key areas: (1) access and networks; (2) inquiry and analysis; and (3) excellence and accountability. The cautions previously put forward about solving any hardware, software or other technological problems of either microcomputers or the Utility itself apply here as well.

1. **Access and Networks**: Assuming that usage costs for the Utility itself are affordable, the Utility, used in tandem with microcomputers,

would make it possible for every building administrator to have on-site access to state of the art hardware at comparatively low cost. Information bases and software also would be made available at reasonable cost.

Unlike many educational innovations which have increased disparity of opportunities in the American school system, the Utility thus would have the potential to decrease disparity by providing access to sophisticated software, broad data bases and up-to-date research findings for all educational administrators. This could be done at a cost which would encourage all districts to participate. Further, it would provide the means for a communication network for educational managers which this group has needed but never enjoyed.

The communication network associated with the Education Utility would provide a unique set of services. For example, such a network would allow educational administrators access to university and federal laboratory-based research at the cutting edge. Research on effective principals, effective schools, effective teaching, information processing, school organizational patterns and so forth has increased in quality and quantity over the past 10 years. At the moment, few administrators routinely can access and interpret this new and growing information base. The Education Utility could set up the first formal communication network between researchers and practitioners by providing updated syntheses of relevant research — updated on virtually a monthly or even more timely basis. This is a specific application of the research updates mentioned in Chapter Two.

Further, in the past two years, educational reform has brought dozens of new field-based initiatives to states across the nation. States such as Illinois, South Carolina and New York are requesting new plans and programs for administrator training, staff evaluation, school reorganization, curriculum reform, differentiated staffing and several other areas. School district managers have had to respond within only months to such new mandates. Often, like islands, districts invent strategies for these initiatives without knowing the responses that other districts are implementing. The Education Utility communication network would permit districts with exemplary programs to share and refine their reform strategies and, at the same time, provide important information to school districts across the nation.

Commercial testing companies and small consulting companies might also have their research, products and services reviewed and inventoried through the Utility. A thesaurus of educational tests, organizational measures and consulting services would increase the efficiency of administrator searches for support services. Presently, there is no single source of information about private sector services and products. The Utility could serve as a means for consumer eduction and brokerage between the two sectors.

No doubt other important types of services and options for administrative practice will emerge as the Utility is developed and used and as access and communication networks proliferate and mature.

2. **Inquiry and Analysis**: While the use of the Education Utility for timely communication with a number of important audiences cannot be underestimated, there also are exciting possibilities in the options for inquiry and analysis offered by sophisticated microcomputer hardware and software technology. These options could, over time, change the way managers think about, monitor and direct the educational process.

In the broadest terms, through the use of the Education Utility, every public school could become an experimenting, laboratory school. Low-cost access to mainframe capacity and cutting-edge software would revolutionize the data bases available to educational managers for informed decision making. The Utility could make available updated information systems on field and university-based research, inventory exemplary programs for use and review by similar districts and provide to all schools the capacity to catalog more and better data on each student. The use of multiple information sources addressing any single educational problem could tend to prevent inappropriate decisions based upon insufficient data bases.

As a primary example, standardized test scores, for more than two decades, have been the single most commonly used measure of achievement in public education. Achievement will continue to be a central focus for researchers and practitioners. However, measures of school success based only upon standardized test scores notoriously are limited in their usefulness to those who manage educational achievement.

To intervene in the instructional process, educational managers also need information about teacher effectiveness, school climate, instructional and learning strategies, students' and teachers' strengths and weaknesses, student learning styles and a whole host of additional variables which describe the learning environment of any given student. In short, administrators need more and better information specific to the level at which they must act to make sound educational decisions. Comparative information from different school settings, such as would be available through the Utility, also would be an invaluable resource for effective decision making in specific situations.

Misuse and non-use of information in the educational system stem from the inaccessibility as well as the reductionist quality of existing data files. It is not easy to identify, for instance, every high risk student in an elementary school based simply on norm-referenced achievement test scores without computer assisted spreadsheet software. It also is not easy to compare the math achievement of bilingual and unilingual students without computer-assisted statistical software. While test data for a single academic year are available for individual students, few teachers have the time, using present technology, to diagnose and then address the learning problems of any single student. They find it difficult to plan their full instructional programs armed only with norm-referenced test data.

Test data are more useful when they are manipulated, broken down into meaningful subgroups and monitored over the length of a student's career. "By hand" data systems, or once-a-year computer analyses purchased from testing companies, do not allow such manipulation. Data are both underused and misused in these situations. However, when teachers, managers and policymakers attempt to collect a broad base of data about the learning environment, they often are "overloaded" with information which cannot be integrated, reconciled or even displayed in a meaningful fashion. Spreadsheets, the working grid provided by microcomputer software, allow educational managers to more easily collect, analyze and display multiple measures of student achievement based upon multiple information sources.

The integrated spreadsheet permits educational managers to scan large data bases quickly in search of relationships among variables. This provides a non-reductionist approach to analyzing educational problems. One type of data, such as test scores on an individual student, would be less likely to misinform when seen in relationship to other, perhaps conflicting, data sources. The integrated spreadsheet would allow a building principal in any district to enter demographic data on each student in the building, and then to add norm-referenced test data, teacher grades, absenteeism and discipline records, special testing results and more. Each year, this file could be updated, allowing for longitudinal analyses. Such a system offers the building administrator an efficient way to survey pupils' progress and to follow the success of special programs and other educational interventions.

In the school building of the future, the educational manager could have at hand a comprehensive and accurate achievement profile on any student in the building. This profile could contain records of all variables considered important by the manager and his or her staff. Additionally, the data could be available over multiple years and analyzed to formulate interventions and assess improvements over time. Grade level and school data could be organized by selected subgroups, tracked over time, and coded to alert staff to achievement problems. At the district level, data could be aggregated and analyzed to guide resource allocations and other decisions. Access to data aggregated across larger units also would be possible through the Education Utility.

At all levels, administrators could access up-to-date research findings in organizational or curricular areas of interest. Communication with other principals across the country with similar problems would be possible. And, on a very timely basis, the building administrator could be measuring and evaluating educational achievement through analytic procedures made possible by the technologies of microcomputers and the Education Utility.

Inquiry and analysis will continue to hold great interest as the tools and technologies to facilitate these activities are developed and implemented. The professional practices of the field of educational administration can be expected to include significantly more and more effective practitioner-initiated inquiry and analysis in the years to come.

3. **Excellence and Accountability**: Educational excellence is an elusive goal. Excellence continues to be redefined as part of the evolutionary process of knowledge development and as a function of our ability to devise an educational system which provides effective avenues to communicate knowledge to young people. We are, however, at a turning point in our ability to improve the quality of educational programs and tailor those programs to the needs of each and every child. With the emergence of integrated information systems, information libraries, curricular support systems and software which could be supported by the Utility, each educational program can be kept current more easily and adapted to school district, school building, classroom or individual student needs.

If educational excellence is defined as the capacity for every educational program to help each child develop his or her talents to the fullest, the application of these new technologies to educational issues and problems will, indeed, foster educational excellence.

Accountability for educational programs likewise will profit from the application of these new technologies. Communication with many audiences on many levels is a key aspect of accountability. At the moment, this is a difficult undertaking but one which will be substantially eased by the ability to "handle" information of the greatest interest to each audience and to pull that information together into meaningful structures.

The whole arena of decision making is a second key element of accountability. Understanding the relationship among different categories of information about educational programs is essential to effective decision making. These relationships will tend to be more clear as information systems become more integrated. For instance, program budgeting, a goal of many educational managers for over two decades, now may be possible. Typically, it has been very difficult to establish the relationship between program cost and program productivity. Yet, making this relationship clear is a cornerstone of accountability. The new information systems described here offer the possibility of looking at multiple measures of program effectiveness and multiple measures of cost so that a far less reductionist view of the relationship between program cost and program productivity can be realized. Again, the key change, made possible by the new technology, is the ability for educational managers to process and act upon a great deal more information without experiencing an information overload.

Our future capabilities to achieve educational excellence and to be accountable for our decisions and actions clearly are tied to advanced technologies associated with microcomputers and the Education Utility. The ultimate impact of these new information system technologies on the schools, and on other educational enterprises, will be determined largely by the willingness of practicing educational administrators to become knowledgeable about the technology. Learning about and applying new information systems will require a substantial effort on their part because these systems will change some fundamental aspects of their professional role. Notably, these new systems both will permit and require that administrators have greater substantive knowledge of the instructional process and broader communication with and about students and teachers and their performance. Some of the complexities and opportunities for training educational administrators in the use of the new information systems and the advanced technologies associated with microcomputers and the Education Utility are explored in a later section of this volume.

It is evident that the Education Utility per se both will fit into current education curricula and practice and will influence the shape of *future* curricula and practices of teaching and administration. The full extent of future changes cannot be adequately understood until experience is gained with the Utility. This chapter has introduced an inventory of possibilities for the future.

On one matter, there can be some agreement: the Education Utility will demand new skills and knowledge from teachers, administrators, learners and parents. How to prepare people to *use* the Utility is taken up in Chapter Five.

CHAPTER FIVE

PREPARING PEOPLE TO USE THE EDUCATION UTILITY

Those who use the Utility must be *prepared* to work with it. Because the Utility opens avenues for instruction and management that have not been available previously, training programs must enable both educators and learners to understand these avenues.

Few educators have had the training necessary for the Education Utility. Further, teacher training programs may not be generally prepared to provide the experiences teachers will need to become effective users of the Utility. A massive effort to develop both preservice training and continuing education on the Utility for teachers and administrators is needed. While such an effort is a substantial undertaking, the developers of the Utility recognize how important this training effort is to the long-range success of the Utility and have made commitments to support the necessary training efforts.

This chapter presents some preliminary thoughts about the preparation of teachers, administrators, parents and learners to use the Utility effectively. Chapter Six, on user support systems, also addresses issues related to training and should be considered in conjunction with Chapter Five. The intent here is not to dictate precisely *how* training should be undertaken but, rather, to indicate the content/substantive issues that might be addressed in the training efforts that will be needed.

Preparing Teachers*

The start of the Education Utility journey coincides with the issuing of a number of reports on American education. Most of these reports inevitably include an examination of the quality and nature of teacher training programs in higher education institutions. The reports touched off a new round of self-examination in most colleges of education, as well as in the halls of state legislatures. Professional associations, accrediting bodies and various ad hoc higher education committees are suggesting new approaches to preparing teachers. Thirty-two states now require, for example, that all those interested in teaching must pass a basic skills examination before they can be admitted into teacher education programs. Some states have passed legislation requiring than an exit test (or "bar" examination, as it is referred to in some states) be given to any graduate of a teacher education program prior to receiving a credential or certification from the state. Some institutions require that students spend five years in teacher education programs. Still others have increased the requirements for more extensive preparation in a discipline in elementary teacher education programs. Teachers in most states must prepare for teaching children with handicapping conditions or must have experience with multicultural educational settings. In some states, graduates of teacher education programs must spend their first professional year as an intern in a school district. In relatively few places prospective teachers must demonstrate basic computer literacy.

All of these efforts are aimed at improving the ability of the teacher to be effective in the classroom. An examination of the typical preparation program, however, reveals that teachers generally are being prepared to work in very traditional classroom settings, with traditional materials and strategies as described in Chapter Four.

But how well do these programs or continuing education efforts prepare teachers for using learning technologies such as the Education Utility? Will "standard" or typical preparation efforts really prepare teachers to exploit the Utility? One can only speculate about the answers, but chances are fairly good that current preparation efforts will *not* prepare teachers adequately for the instructional possibilities and problems presented by the Education Utility. If this is correct, what changes might need to be made in teacher preparation programs?

First, we need to identify the knowledge and/or skills that a teacher

---

* Contributions to this section were made by Dr. John McLevie, Associate Dean, School of Education, University of Houston/Clear Lake.

might need to use the Education Utility. As stated earlier, it is not the intent here to discuss *how* nor *when* skills should be taught. In general, teacher education ought to be conceived of as an *ongoing* process, where there is a clear and continuing connection between preservice and continuing education programs. It is likely that preparation for the Utility also will be an ongoing process, throughout the professional career of a teacher or administrator, as he or she develops ever more sophistication in its uses. Educators ought to be the epitome of lifelong learners!

(Paranthetically, the Utility itself ought to be heavily used to deliver continuing education to teachers.)

Given those caveats, the following are areas in which teachers might need to be prepared if they are to use the Education Utility reflectively:

The classics of teacher education

Much of the content of current teacher education programs should continue to be included in the preparation of teachers for classrooms of the future. For example, all teachers should have a strong sense of the historical development of the field of education, and of some of the philosophical patterns and/or principles in American education. Teachers should have a grasp of the basic concepts of learning and human development and of curriculum theory and development. In addition, teachers would profit from understanding some of the emerging theories of instruction and instructional design and development.

It also is essential that anyone seeking a career as a teacher have a strong preparation in an appropriate discipline or disciplines. This applies to elementary as well as secondary teachers. As suggested above, more and more prospective elementary teachers are being required to concentrate in one or two discipline areas, as well as in the range of content areas they are expected to teach to elementary children.

In some programs, students are required to gain at least an initial understanding of concepts of measurement and testing, and some programs expect undergraduate students to develop an understanding of methods of inquiry. These skill areas are vital to the teacher working with the Utility and should be emphasized in any teacher's general preparation.

Most teacher education programs now require preparation in multicultural education, special education and other topical areas that reflect the realities of many American classrooms. Those experiences are valuable in general and may be particularly important in class-rooms where the Utility is available.

These "classical" dimensions of teacher education programs, where taught knowledgeably and enthusiastically, are essential for anyone wishing to be a teacher. They also are necessary for teachers being prepared to use the Education Utility. But the Utility also may require preparation not now included in most teacher education programs.

Mastering the mechanics and tools of the Utility

If the Utility is to be fully utilized teachers will need to become intimately familiar with the mechanics of how to use it, and particularly with the various instructional and analytical tools it will make available to teachers and learners.

As explained in Chapter Two, the Utility is being designed so the user does not need to be a specialized technician. The Utility is to be extremely "user friendly" and its technology "transparent." None-theless, it will be important for teachers to be able to handle basic aspects of the system (how to get in and out, how to print materials, how to find them, etc.). Many teachers are intimidated by technology, afraid they will be embarrassed or frustrated when trying to make it work. Teachers must feel comfortable with the mechanics of the Utility in order to make it work for them. Too often, this part of the training of teachers has been taken for granted, resulting in teachers refusing to use available technologies. The Utility, on the surface, may appear complex. Teachers need to know that it isn't.

Users of the Utility will have access to the variety of tools described in Chapter Two. These will be extremely valuable to the teacher, but, once again, teachers must be adequately prepared to use them or they simply will sit idle. For example: various word processing and spreadsheet programs will be available, making it possible for teachers to accomplish many tasks, but *only* if they receive adequate instructions and preparation in the how and why of these tools.

The Utility also will include resources uniquely valuable to teachers. One of the most powerful will be the curriculum alignment package, as described in Chapters Two and Four. This package will enable teachers to select or develop learning objectives or goals, identify programs and materials in the Utility especially designed to match those goals or objectives, and choose test items or procedures to assess how students achieve specific objectives. This alignment process will enable teachers to develop and provide to learners individualized education. This major feature of the Utility will require specific training.

As teachers gain experience with the various tools on the Utility, they will be able to expand their application in various contexts. Initial training of teachers to use these tools is, however, critical because if it is neglected, most teachers never will avail themselves of the power of the Utility.

The characteristics of learners

One of the classic elements in the preparation of teachers is the area of human development and learning. Teachers need to know how people learn and how they develop over time.

The Education Utility, however, introduces a somewhat more complex need for information about learning. As was pointed out in Chapter Four, individualizing instruction requires the teacher to know a great deal *about* each student, a fact which mitigated against previous efforts to individualize instruction. The Utility makes it possible for the teacher to develop and then use for instructional purposes a more complicated learner profile. Teachers will need to learn some new skills to develop and use such profiles.

To summarize Chapter Four's description of individual student profiles, the Utility will permit the teacher to aggregate data on variables such as:

1. Performance on specific instructional activities;
2. Performance on a range of tests or other measures of learning outcomes;
3. Data related to cognitive styles;
4. Data on family background;
5. Records of books read, activities undertaken, etc.;
6. Other information on student performance on very specific tasks, standardized tests, and other assessments.

The Utility will enable the teacher to track the student's progress through an instructional program and to determine if the student requires remediation, special attention, etc. Based on the profile developed by aggregating student information of this kind, the teacher will be better able to develop learning programs for each student. The *mechanical* burden of recording such data will be relieved from the teacher, freeing him or her to evaluate the *meaning* of the information at hand.

Teachers most often receive, at best, minimum training in tests and measurement during their preservice program. Some take additional coursework in their graduate programs that may be useful in gathering and interpreting information about students. Generally, however, their preparation in this area is limited, and needs to be improved.

The Education Utility allows teachers to both gather and analyze a much wider range of information about learner characteristics and performance than has been true in the past. Theoretically, the Utility ought to make available to the teacher information that will make it possible to design individualized programs. But teachers first must have specific training in gathering and using information useful in shaping individualized programs. At a conceptual level, many questions need to be raised about such information, including: What ought to be included in such a profile? How is that information best obtained? What kinds of information influence instructional decisions? Teachers need to know how to use the data gathering and aggregating capacities of the Utility which still are being developed.

But the most critical skill in assessment will be the ability of the teacher to interpret information about individual learners and/or groups of learners and use that information for decisions about instructional strategies and/or materials. Training in this skill is not a trivial matter. While research mentioned earlier will be helpful, experience with the Utility will illuminate this issue much more. One thing is certain: an integrated approach to a school's information management system is essential if the Utility is to realize its potential.

Designing instructional sessions

Teachers who work with the Education Utility will need quite different lesson planning skills. Most preparation programs teach how to develop lesson or curriculum plans. These generally include instructional objectives, learning activities, materials to be used, content to be taught and evaluation procedures to be used in a given lesson. The lesson plans provide fairly broad outlines of what teachers will attempt to accomplish during a given time period, or instructional session.

Teachers using the Utility also will need to prepare lesson plans but the *content* may be a bit different. Teachers will be able to design both individualized and group or class instructional plans, meshing the two. Such planning may sound complicated, but fortunately the teacher can look to the Utility itself for help in doing this kind of instructional planning. The curriculum alignment capabilities of the Utility, for example, will be invaluable to the teacher attempting to design sessions for both individual and group work. Other instructional planning tools will undoubtedly emerge as more experience is gained with the Utility.

To design individualized study, teachers will need to refine their skills in specifying what they want learners to learn and/or experience, such as teachers must do *without* the Utility. With the Utility's power, however, the teacher must be more skillful in relating instructional strategies and resources to learner characteristics and learning styles, as suggested in Chapter Four.

Accessing resources

Because the Utility provides a much greater choice of instructional resources than currently available, both learners and teachers will need to know how to access them.

Teachers must learn what is available through the Utility. They will need to develop skills in catergorizing or identifying the materials they need, not a simple task in itself. Teachers also will have to develop effective *search* skills, that is, those needed to thoroughly search through the Utility system for materials and programs germane to a particular instructional objective or learner. The indices provided by the Utility will help, as will tools such as the curriculum alignment procedures. Teachers must be comfortable using both indices and tools.

Teachers also will need considerable skills in selecting and evaluating instructional resources. Some attention to developing these skills is included in many teacher education programs but may need to be emphasized more in the future. It is not sufficient for the resources to be available through the Utility; the teacher must be able to evaluate them carefully for any given instructional task and to select the most appropriate materials for a learner or a group. Again, some of the tools on the Utility will help, but teachers will need to make many more material and program choices than in "regular" classrooms.

Teachers will also need to identify materials and/or programs *not* currently in the Utility system. The Utility is designed to be responsive to learner and teacher needs. Materials cannot be added unless teachers or others identify specific needs for them. Being able to recognize when something is missing and to describe materials and/or programs that should be added to the Utility system are not, of course, routine activities of teachers. They will need training in how to specify clearly their program or materials needs.

Of course, teachers working *without* the Utility make decisions about instructional resources. All teachers spend time and effort searching out appropriate instructional resources for their students. The Education Utility, however, promises to make significantly greater numbers and kinds of resources available to every teacher. The potential inherent in more and different resources will be realized only if individual teachers use those resources in efficient and effective ways. New skills may be needed to do this.

Classroom management skills

Teachers must know how to manage classrooms. In traditional teacher preparation programs, classroom management is about discipline, how to keep order. Such a focus is very appropriate because in some schools maintaining a sense of order is a major undertaking. In the classroom of the future, management also will be a concern of the teacher, but the *kind* of classroom management needed where the Utility is at work may be different from conventional classrooms.

Discipline always will be an issue, of course, because of the nature of the young. The teacher using the Utility, however, must understand how to manage a classroom where 30 students might very well be engaged in 30 different tasks. Traditional problems of maintaining discipline well might give way to problems of managing a lot of individual learning programs. This project may be more *pleasant*, but, nonetheless, difficult to manage.

Classroom management with the Utility, where the teacher must be a master coordinator, means knowing how and when to be available to students and how to connect them to work on common problems or projects. Classroom management thus becomes much more of an *instructional* management challenge than a discipline-maintaining one. The proportion of a teacher's time devoted to behavior management, as compared to instructional management, is likely to be much less in classrooms with the Utility, but most teachers will need new skills to handle their new management challenges.

Teaching learners tool skills

Teachers themselves may need to learn a host of new "tool" skills to use the Utility, such as effective typing or use of word processing and spreadsheet programs. Teachers also will need to teach students these skills. This teaching will need to become a part of the curriculum, primarily at the elementary school level, but later grades may include more advanced tool skills.

Using networks

The Education Utility will permit and indeed encourage networks of learners with other teachers, learners with teachers, teachers with other teachers, parents with teachers or teachers with administrators. The networking capabilities of the Education Utility are powerful and fascinating and could have far-reaching social implications. Furthermore, such networks are so new that not a lot is known about how to use them for instruction.

Teachers will be involved very heavily in creating many of these networks. For example: a teacher may encourage a seventh grade student in Akron, Ohio, working on a project on volcanoes, to communicate by electronic mail with a student living near a volcano in Hawaii, to enhance perceptions the Ohio student forms from her reading. The student might also contact, via the Utility, a professor in a university to discuss the history of volcanic activity. In this instance, the teacher first will encourage the student to attempt a network, then help find the personal resources through the Utility. The teacher also will help with the mechanics of the network and receive feedback from the student about the "electronic conversation." Such network possibilities are fascinating but will not be used appropriately unless teachers are trained to consider how networking will contribute to instructional programming.

Similarly, teachers need to join networks with other teachers. The Utility could serve as a valuable source of continuing professional education for each teacher, as well as a means of reducing the isolation within which most teachers work. Here again, teachers need to be made aware of these possibilities and learn how to initiate networks.

Home interactions

Unfortunately, many teacher preparation programs fail to include, as part of their curriculum, adequate attention to how teachers should involve the families of students. Most teachers report their preparation in this area is at best minimal, and at worst nonexistent.

The Utility opens up possibilities for new kinds of teacher-home interaction. For example, students, through home terminals and a local telephone call, will be able to dial into the Utility to continue work they bring home from school. Teachers could communicate directly with parents through the Utility. In return, parents could communicate with the school (or other parents, experts, etc.) through their own network on the Utility, monitor the work their children are doing in school, and learn how to be better partners in learning.

Teachers will need to develop new attitudes, and possibly new skills, in interacting with the families of students. Just what those skills might be is still unclear, but we do know the Utility could make such relationships more feasible.

Content / context / goal specific instructional strategies

Finally, it may be useful to discuss briefly the need to prepare teachers to use the Utility specifically for certain content, context or instructional goals. The skills outlined above are *generic*, skills that cut across subject matter or contextual lines. In addition, however, teachers may need to develop skills specific to certain content or certain educational settings.

For example: The Utility may present opportunities for the use of highly creative programming to teach mathematical concepts. In most teacher preparation programs, prospective elementary teachers receive some introduction to math "methods," while secondary education students are likely to learn somewhat more, but not always adequate, methods of instruction unique to mathematics. The Utility may require even more (or different) mathematics methods to be taught to prospective teachers. Without more specialized instructional methods geared to the use of the Utility, the teacher may fail to use the instructional power of the Utility in mathematics.

Chapter Six contains a proposal for demonstration centers for both research/development and training. One or more of these demonstration centers could focus on creating materials and strategies for a given content or contextual domain. Some teachers will want advanced training in methods for these domains, which the centers should provide.

The skills teachers need to effectively use the Education Utility in some ways will be different from those required by teachers in today's elementary and secondary classrooms. And yet, one of the most fundamental teaching skills — that of adequately conceptualizing both the ideas to be taught in a given lesson and the ways to teach those ideas — will be as important in the classroom of the future as it is today. This requires clarity of thinking about what one hopes students to achieve. Teachers who lack this skill tend to lose much learning time for students and confuse them about what they are expected to accomplish. As a result teachers and students often become disillusioned about schooling. In many ways, the Utility will demand even more clarity on the part of teachers.

Another quality needed by an excellent teacher is a sensitivity to and understanding of individual children and adolescents, enabling the teachers to craft instruction to the level of the student. The effective use of the Education Utility will certainly require this sensitivity. The good sense of the "natural" teacher will be as important when using the Utility as it has ever been. There can be little doubt that more use of technology is imminent in our society and in our schools. The effective teacher must make that technology humane.

It would be tragic if the Utility were to be used only as a source of facts and data gathering, as often seems to be the emphasis in the use of technology today. The potential for the Utility in heightening the conceptual and critical thinking of students is great. Teachers must learn to work with higher order thinking skills of students, a goal often espoused but too seldom accomplished.

Critics claim that classroom teaching lags behind current research findings about effective instruction, takes little advantage of existing technology and is unclear about goals and objectives. At least part of the blame for this perception is leveled at teachers and, in turn, at teacher preparation efforts. The Education Utility could bring new power and resources to the task of helping teachers develop new instructional methods.

Preparing Educational Administrators*

In Chapter Four, several implications of the Education Utility for educational administration and management were described. Educational administration must develop new, comprehensive and integrated computer-based information systems to better coordinate and, therefore, improve educational management. Such information systems are prerequisite to more meaningful educational accountability and educational quality. These new information systems offer extraordinary potential to better integrate information for educational decision making across six essential areas: student, personnel, instructional, fiscal, organizational and information management.

New information systems are fundamentally central to increased management effectiveness. And, advanced technologies associated with microcomputers and the Education Utility are central to improved information systems. Because of recent developments in the hardware and software of these technologies, we are now, in fact, in the midst of an information systems revolution that will profoundly affect educational practice and management. The Education Utility, having appeared during this revolution, has the capability to facilitate the implementation of integrated information systems in education and to shape a number of information system components.

For the field of educational administration to join and lead this revolution in education, intensive new efforts to train educational administrators in microcomputer and Education Utility concepts and technologies are essential. This section focuses on three dimensions of this new training:

* This section was contributed by Muriel E. Mackett, Frederick P. Frank, Jeri Nowakoski, and Peter Abrams, College of Education, Northern Illinois University. The authors draw on the thinking presented in their contribution in Chapter 4 and on their experience in providing training in integrated information systems for administrators in Illinois.

- **The current mandate for revised administrator training**. This includes a brief examination of links between administrator accountability for effective schools and application of new information technologies to educational and management practice.
- **Frameworks for administrator training**. This proposes training in information technologies at awareness, user proficiency and problem solving/application levels. Proposed training content is based on the need for administrators to manage integrated information systems. This calls for six information systems elements (student, personnel, instructional, fiscal, organizational, and information management) and eight traditional management task areas (planning, organizing, staffing/supervising, directing, coordinating, reporting, budgeting and evaluating*).
- **Implementation of training**. This includes brief discussions of planning and resources necessary to get revised administrator training underway.

The Mandate for Revising Administrator Training

The emergence of advanced technologies associated with microcomputers and the Education Utility is both important and timely. Largely as a result of the impact of recent reports on education, administrators are under heavy pressure from many segments of society to provide the leadership necessary for "more effective schools." But while administrators must respond to this mandate, interpretations of the meaning of the term "more effective schools" are diverse, often unclear and even contradictory. Administrator response also is made more difficult by:

- Substantial decreases in resources available to support education;
- Continuing problems, such as student dropouts and substance abuse, an aging teacher cadre and teacher "burnout" and unequal educational opportunity for various at-risk student populations; and
- Unrealistic expectations shared by many that educational institutions can and should bear major responsibility for solving social problems.

Yet, the challenge of creating increased educational effectiveness and management accountability through the technologies of microcomputers and the Education Utility is one of the more optimistic immediate prospects for administrators. Of the many technological innovations which one could predict might succeed in education, integrated computer-based information systems would seem to be among the most feasible, promising and far reaching.

Effective application of these new information technologies will require that administrators fundamentally change how they define and carry out many of their management responsibilities. Equally important, school board members, teachers and other education professionals also will need to participate in the evolution of administrator responsibilities resulting from using new and expanded computer-based information systems. Specifically, we believe this evolution in administrative practice will be driven by a recognition of four crucial points.

First, the present education structure may have reached the limits of "traditional" information systems technologies. Traditional "by hand" information systems, even with mainframe support, have not increased the effectiveness of educational management because thus far they have not bridged the dichotomy between instructional management and other management functions. The aggressive application of new information systems technologies offers a chance to explore management alternatives and, hopefully, to better understand, integrate and use information about all facets of schooling.

Second, implementation of the concepts and technologies associated with integrated information systems, microcomputers and the Education Utility can be expected to create new standards for management accountability. Management practices which were once only abstract possibilities or undertaken at the option of the administrator will become an accepted expectation and standard. For example, even a principal in a small isolated school would be able to have access to the latest research and to review exemplary programs through a national computer network made feasible by the new technologies. Whole new repertoires of management practices will become concrete and application of new technologies will become expected and then routine. Educational administrators should take the lead in this movement, helping to develop the full potential of these technologies to benefit educational practice.

Third, an important facet of revised training for educational administrators will be its capability to bridge the gap between existing management knowledge and skills and the new knowledge and skills necessary for sophisticated information technologies. Many practices now associated with effective educational administration will continue to be useful. The training task ahead essentially is one of refining current management practices to accommodate new possibilities, reshaping past practices to take advantage of new technologies and literally developing new domains of information management and decision making practices. These transitions will not be accomplished easily, cheaply or quickly. Nevertheless, as application of new computer-information technologies takes place and new standards for educational practice and accountability evolve, it increasingly will become clear that management practices throughout education must change to accommodate new possibilities. Effective training in the new information technologies will be essential for administrators to participate in and lead this movement.

Fourth, questions about the content of revised administrator training efforts must be addressed promptly and systematically. Information systems technologies will continue to develop and expand, requiring that the content of administrator training programs be revised. Research and evaluation efforts to provide feedback about training content and the effects of particular kinds of training on administrator effectiveness therefore should be undertaken as an integral part of revised administrator training efforts. But appropriate content for administrator training also is of immediate concern because of state mandates for revised administrator training and, in many cases, changing certification requirements. The sense of urgency about getting revised training underway could lead to poorly designed and delivered inservice and preservice training of administrators. Training content issues, then, are crucial.

Frameworks for Administrator Training

Neither the scope of the retraining effort, nor ambiguities over the best agenda for training nor training costs can be allowed to distract from developing coherent training goals and short- and long-term strategies to achieve those goals. These tasks will be made easier when those responsible for training have gained first-hand experience with the new information technologies and can see their many potential benefits for education.

As described earlier, the application of integrated information systems to student, personnel, instructional, fiscal, organizational and information management practices will improve educational practice significantly. The core application of new information technology is, in fact, information management. But the key to effective long-term application of computer technology rests with careful thinking about the meaning of the information and reasons for gathering it in the first place.

Clearly, the purpose of information management is to promote informed decision making and therefore more "effective schools." But systematic training efforts in the new information technologies that relate to day-to-day administrator decision making have not yet appeared. A framework describing such training is proposed here. It incorporates two primary elements: (1) training scope and (2) training content. It is assumed throughout that efforts to "train the trainers" would need to be undertaken, primarily by colleges of education, as part of an overall training strategy.

1. **Training Scope**: Efforts to train administrators in the concepts, technologies and applications of integrated information systems, microcomputers and the Education Utility should be planned to accommodate a wide scope of training needs. Training needs have three levels — awareness, user proficiency, and problem solving/application. These training levels are interrelated rather than strictly sequential.

First, *awareness level training* should provide administrators with the opportunity to see how the new computer technologies function and how they might influence management practices. Administrators would need descriptions of microcomputer and Education Utility technologies and how they interface. In many, if not most cases, this would require communicating basic information about microcomputers; software, such as word processing, spreadsheets and statistical programs; information systems applications; and how these systems will evolve in the future. The basic awareness skills are similar to those needed by teachers. Administrators also would need basic training in the concepts behind the new information systems described here, how these systems tie to microcomputer and Utility technologies and implications for educational practices and accountability.

Second, direct hands-on training should be provided at the *user level* so that administrators become proficient in actually using the technologies for a variety of educational purposes. At a minimum, administrators would need to learn:

- Word processing;
- On-site data entry and retrieval;
- Linkage and networking functions both on-site and in the Utility network;
- How to manage access and input to the library of resources and data banks expected to be available through the Utility;
- How to use the technologies in alternative education delivery systems, including interfaces with home and community;
- How to carry out inquiry and applied research;
- How to carry out statistical procedures for analyzing on-site and larger data banks (meta analysis);
- How to manage information across major management functions (student, personnel, instructional, fiscal, and organizational management);
- How to undertake strategic planning and follow up;

- How to allocate and manage resources to support implementation of the technologies; and
- How to communicate about these systems to educational professionals and laypersons.

Proficiency in several other areas no doubt would be required as well. Training in all content or skill areas would be essential if administrators are to use the new technologies effectively. This especially is true at the building level where principals are, in effect, in charge of most clerical, data collection and data analysis functions. Heavy reliance on typical clerical support to carry out these functions likely would not provide the quality of assistance required to use an information system to best advantage. The administrator most likely to understand and use information management effectively will be the one who is proficient at accessing and manipulating information through computers and the Education Utility.

Third, training at the *problem solving/application level* also should be provided so administrators develop the capacity to anticipate and help create applications of microcomputer and Utility technologies to educational practice. Specifically, administrators should learn how to apply the new computer technologies to current management practices. As these technologies are integrated more fully into management thinking, their potential to alter management practices will be realized.

If the new information technologies are to be useful, administrators must understand enough about the technologies to apply them to emerging management problems. By integrating these technologies with knowledge of educational operations, administrators could forge new domains of management practice. A primary focus of these efforts should be on integrating instructional management and other management functions.

The full scope of administrator training needs at the levels of awareness, user proficiency and problem solving/application require immediate attention. Broad-scale efforts, designed to train large numbers of current administrators in a relatively short time (perhaps within two to three years), should be undertaken as quickly as possible. Parallel efforts should be undertaken, as well, to include appropriate training in preservice administrator preparation programs. Ongoing, permanent attention will be necessary to enable all administrators to keep pace with rapid changes in information systems technologies.

Training should not and need not proceed in any strictly sequential fashion from awareness, to user proficiency, to problem solving/application levels. Our experience with actual integrated information systems training programs with practicing administrators is that training can be structured so that beginning phases of each training level occur essentially at the same time and advance in tandem. Administrators undergoing district-supported information systems training can move very quickly through essential beginning awareness and user proficiency level material so that some problem solving applications using the new technologies can be integrated into training early on. This can be done in a matter of days if the training program is sufficiently intense.

Again, our experience indicates that as administrators begin to see how use of the technologies relates to real school problems and to decisions they must make, they become highly motivated to expand their skills to support their problem solving and decision making needs. Greater problem solving and application capabilities develop over time, contributing to more effective decision making. Practicing administrators not only advance quickly but also enjoy doing so. Presumably, similar results also would be obtained in pre-service administrator training programs.

Whether inservice or preservice training aimed at large groups of administrators could be conducted using this approach, or with similar effects, is open to question. In any case, the full scope of training needs at awareness, user proficiency and problem solving/application training levels should be central to the effort to train administrators in the new technologies and should be treated in as integrated a fashion as possible.

2. **Training Content**: The essential point to be made about content for revised administrator training programs is that it is *not* simply a question of learning about how to use the new information technologies. Clearly, this must occur, but this aspect of training is by far the easiest. The most difficult, challenging and essential part of revised administrator training is learning to apply these technologies to the complexities of educational and education management practices that are part of the fabric of the educational process.

For our purposes, we have chosen to illustrate this point by juxtaposing two related domains of administration — the six information systems elements for which administrators are responsible (student, personnel, instructional, fiscal, organizational and information management) and eight day-to-day administrator task areas (planning, organizing, staffing/supervising, directing, coordinating, reporting, budgeting and evaluating). Figure 5 displays an integrated spreadsheet format and attempts to demonstrate the relationship between the new information technologies, educational information systems, administrator task areas and proposed training content.

A single example of applied links between information systems elements and administrator task areas is shown in Figure 5 at the intersection of *planning* and *student management* (cell A1). Analogous applied links within each of the remaining 47 cells in the figure are assumed. Information links which integrate all 48 cells also are noted:

- Without new, integrated information systems technologies for the six information systems elements and the eight task areas, administrators tend to treat these as fairly separate functions or tasks.
- Because the new microcomputer and Utility information technologies facilitate unprecedented low-cost data storage, access, analysis and manipulation, administrators who use these technologies should have the capability to more fully integrate the six information elements into a unified system, to better coordinate administrative work across the eight task areas and to integrate all of these tasks across a unified information system (consistent with the 48 cells implied in the figure). This means that tasks and information which apply in any one cell link to and have an impact on tasks and information which apply in virtually all other cells.
- This application of new information technologies to educational and management practice should contribute to increased management accountability for more effective schools and define the parameters of content for revised administrator training.

Clearly then, the content of revised administrator training should include the awareness and user proficiency levels described previously but must focus on developing requisite knowledge and skills for effective application of information technologies within and across information system elements and administrative task areas. Two additional points are important in this regard.

First, the six essential elements of integrated information systems for educational management incorporate a full range of management functions:

- *Student management* includes managing student performance and progress, recordkeeping and scheduling.
- *Personnel management* includes personnel selection, development and evaluation, and inservice training.
- *Instructional management* includes management of teaching and learning processes and instructional and curricular materials, as well as curriculum and program development and evaluation.
- *Fiscal management* includes accounting, budgeting and resource allocation.
- *Organizational management* includes reporting, decision making, planning and accountability.

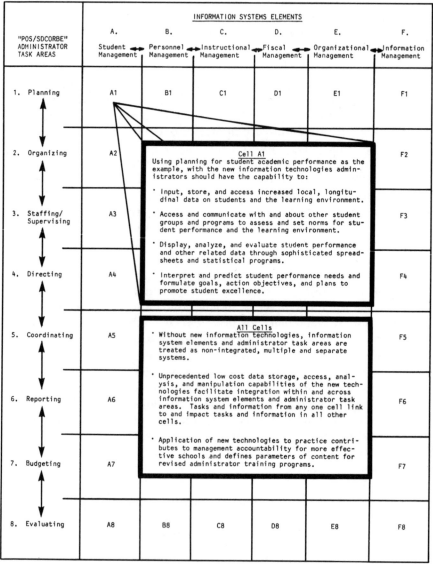

| | INFORMATION SYSTEMS ELEMENTS ||||||
"POS/SDCORBE" ADMINISTRATOR TASK AREAS	A. Student Management	B. Personnel Management	C. Instructional Management	D. Fiscal Management	E. Organizational Management	F. Information Management
1. Planning	A1	B1	C1	D1	E1	F1
2. Organizing	A2					F2
3. Staffing/ Supervising	A3					F3
4. Directing	A4					F4
5. Coordinating	A5					F5
6. Reporting	A6					F6
7. Budgeting	A7					F7
8. Evaluating	A8	B8	C8	D8	E8	F8

Cell A1

Using planning for student academic performance as the example, with the new information technologies administrators should have the capability to:

* Input, store, and access increased local, longitudinal data on students and the learning environment.

* Access and communicate with and about other student groups and programs to assess and set norms for student performance and the learning environment.

* Display, analyze, and evaluate student performance and other related data through sophisticated spreadsheets and statistical programs.

* Interpret and predict student performance needs and formulate goals, action objectives, and plans to promote student excellence.

All Cells

* Without new information technologies, information system elements and administrator task areas are treated as non-integrated, multiple and separate systems.

* Unprecedented low cost data storage, access, analysis, and manipulation capabilities of the new technologies facilitate integration within and across information system elements and administrator task areas. Tasks and information from any one cell link to and impact tasks and information in all other cells.

* Application of new technologies to practice contributes to management accountability for more effective schools and defines parameters of content for revised administrator training programs.

Integrated Spreadsheet of Information Systems Elements and POS/SDCORBE Administrator Task Areas

Modified from Gulick, Luther and L. Urwick, eds., Papers *On The Science of Administration*, New York: Institute of Public Administration, 1937.

"POSDCoRB" refers to Planning, Organizing, Staffing, Directing, Coordinating, Reporting and Budgeting. Again, see Gulick, Luther and L. Urwick, eds., *Papers on the Science of Administration*, New York: Institute of Public Administration, 1937.

Figure 5

• *Information management* includes the knowledge, skills and procedures for establishing, maintaining, developing, accessing, analyzing and utilizing information.

When the content of revised administrator training in new information technologies is considered in terms of these elements, it is
evident there are large and fairly well developed bodies of knowledge
about each of them. But it is equally evident that the literature is
not well integrated *across* these elements. Graduate courses for example, tend to be specialized and might not even touch on all of the
management areas in any one course. Virtually all administrators (as
well as other education professionals) have major gaps in their
individual and collective grasp of these management areas and their
interrelationships. To some extent this is a natural reflection of
individual talents and experiences. But to a much greater extent,
these gaps reflect lack of integration in the literature, practice in the
field and training in educational administrator preparation programs.
These gaps tend to be most severe in the areas of information
management and instructional management. Gaps in knowledge of
instructional management are of greater concern because instruction
is so fundamental to what we expect will be administrators' future
responsibilities for developing and applying integrated information
systems. Addressing gaps in both of these areas (information and
instructional management) should be an important part of revised
administrator training programs. Appropriate corresponding development of administrator knowledge and skill in student, personnel,
fiscal and organizational management should also be central to these
training efforts. The importance of structuring training and defining
training content along these lines should not be underestimated; they
will assure that administrators have the capability to develop and
apply integrated information systems to practice.
Second, although skills in the eight administrator task areas shown
in Figure 5 are typically high among many practitioners, there still
is a strong need for training that links the task areas to new information
technologies. These areas include: planning, organizing, staffing/
supervising, directing, coordinating, reporting, budgeting and evaluating and are based on Luther Gulick's classic and still applicable
"POSDCoRB" model, which we have modified liberally by redefining task areas and adding "Supervision" and "Evaluation." (Thus,
these can be referred to as "POS/SDCoRBE." We have chosen and
modified this model precisely because the language is commonly
understood in studies of administration and because the POS/
SDCoRBE task areas cut across or apply to each of the six elements
of integrated information systems as shown in Figure 5.

Each of the POS/SDCoRBE task areas are defined and briefly discussed below. Problems with which administrators must deal in carrying out tasks are described and implications of information systems technologies for addressing these problems are explained. Two key implications of the new technologies apply across all eight task areas: (1) they increase the capacity to use multiple measures to inform decision making; and (2) they increase the capacity to gather and analyze information at lower cost. This is in contrast to traditional management practice, which has tended to rely on fewer information sources to support decision making in task areas because information costs have tended to be too high.

Planning is defined as the process of specifying long range organizational goals and action objectives and means to achieve them. In the absence of new information technologies, typical organizational planning efforts center more on short-range rather than long-range goals and objectives. Traditional management technologies tend to produce quite limited and short term information bases. The data available for planning tasks often cannot be aggregated meaningfully across organizational levels or management decision areas; that is, student, personnel, instructional, fiscal and organizational areas. Administrators, thus, have limited ability to analyze or manipulate data in ways that help them to see long-range organizational needs.

With the new information systems technologies, it should be possible for administrators to have access to more comprehensive data bases, catalogue data more representative of their needs and treat the data longitudinally. Of utmost importance is the notion that data important to successful planning can be gathered as part of the ongoing activity of the organization. The sheer volume of data that administrators will be able to use for planning should be increased exponentially. Administrators will, therefore, have at hand a vastly increased potential to undertake more complex analyses and predictions of long-term organizational needs to specify long range goals and action objectives and to formulate plans to achieve them.

Organizing is defined as the process of determining the formal structure of the organization and designing task areas, staff assignments and resource allocation and use. In large part because of the structures and fairly inflexible character of the information produced through traditional management technologies, administrators (and others) tend to see and treat the formal structure of the organization as inflexible. It is often difficult, in the absence of alternative information patterns, for administrators to envision options for how the educational organization might be structured to carry out its work.

With the more comprehensive and integrated information produced by the new information systems technologies, administrators should see more room for flexibility within the organizational structure and envision alternative delivery options. Administrators should have access to and be able to "handle" more and better information about the instructional process and student and staff performance, for example. This should provide the bases for more integrated views of the organization and for them to perceive the whole organization as more manageable. This should promote greater organization of the schools on the basis of structures, task areas, staff assignments and resource use that reflect individual needs and differences.

Staffing / supervising is defined as the process of recruiting, selecting, training, monitoring and rewarding or remediating staff as needed. Typical problems which administrators face in staffing and supervising also center around limitations in the current information base. Currently, information available to administrators suitable for diagnosing staffing/supervising needs is extremely limited. Administrators also have limited capability to provide for differentiated staff roles due to "institutionalized" inflexibility in the organizational structure. Also, costs of carrying out clinical supervision programs without efficient information systems for evaluation decisions and staff development efforts are very high.

With the new information systems technologies, administrators should be able to better and more accurately assess current and future staffing and supervising needs, thus leading to more reliable and effective selection, training and use of personnel. This information should also offer a much needed and useful data base for communication about student and staff performance, instruction and curriculum and many other aspects of the organization — across roles, classroom, schools and districts. This information and communication also should lead to development of new kinds of staff development programs. The pool of potential personnel from which administrators are able to select job candidates should also increase substantially through the use of a broad-based staff registry system available at state and national levels.

Directing is defined as the use of leadership and authority to manage personnel and provide instructions for action. Typical problems now faced by administrators when carrying out the directing task include the lack of well-developed feedback systems which would offer systematic, timely and adequately specific information about the quality of organizational functioning and organizational and staff needs. The directing task is commonly undertaken in a climate of ambiguity and uncertainty about what instructions for action should be given and to what ends. Administrators too often must rely on position authority rather than on leadership based on shared information to accomplish organizational goals.

With the new information systems technologies, administrators can expect to have systematic, timely and adequately specific information at their disposal regarding many aspects of organizational functioning. This information should enable administrators to develop a clearer sense of organizational needs and to use more systematic approaches to directing the organization. To the extent that greater numbers of system personnel can have access to a more comprehensive and integrated information base, there should also be an increase in shared, informed decision making.

Coordinating is defined as the process of interrelating the various parts of the organization and its services. The most serious problems which administrators now face in carrying out the coordinating task relate to artificial separations between organizational functions occurring as a result of the lack of an integrated information base. The coordinating function often is limited to mere sharing of human and financial resources because the information to reach more effective and efficient resource allocation decisions is not present. Coordination within schools, across schools within a district and across districts that would maximize use of resources and quality of organizational services is frequently absent or very limited.

With the new information systems technologies, the presence of good information should promote more effective decision making about the coordinating task. This should lead to better linking and integrating of organizational functions as well as the resources needed to support those functions within and across schools and districts. Organizational services therefore should be delivered more efficiently and effectively. Coordination at state and national levels also becomes a possibility through the networking capability of the Education Utility.

Reporting is defined as the process of keeping staff, stake holders and governing bodies informed, through records, research and other elements of the information system, about the functioning and health of the organization, including student performance. Currently, the reporting function is tied to information bases which tend to be narrow, limited and short-range. The information collected tends to be driven by external reporting requirements and most often is descriptive rather than analytic. Reporting, therefore, typically consumes very large amounts of resources without addressing specific needs for information most appropriate for communication with staff, stake holders and governing bodies. Reporting is also typically separated from decision making and action when these should, in fact, be closely tied together.

With the new information systems technologies, reporting should in large part become integrated with governing the organization and tracking student performance for instructional decision making. The new technologies should increase the quality and usefulness of the information available and do so more cost efficiently and effectively. These systems also will allow for more complex analyses and interpretations of data to inform decision making and actions and for appropriate communication about organizational functioning, including student performance, with staff, stake holders and governing bodies.

Budgeting is defined as fiscal planning, accounting, accountability and control. With traditional management technologies, information for budgeting decisions tends to be fragmented and separated from information about program needs. The procedures for collecting budgetary information also tend to place budgeting decisions too much in the hands of single administrators. Because the available information is not integrated across decision or program areas, these administrators are not and cannot be expected to adequately tie budgeting decisions to program needs, that is, to use resources in ways that maximize cost effectiveness and program quality.

With the new information systems technologies, it should be possible for administrators to develop fully integrated program budgeting and fiscal planning, accounting, accountability and control systems. Because of the networking features of the new technologies, the budgeting process also should be more broadly based in the future. These changes should promote increased cost effectiveness and program quality.

Evaluating is defined as the process of assessing the worth of organizational services for purposes of improvement and accountability. Currently, the data bases available for carrying out the evaluating task tend to be over-simplified relative to the complexity of the educational process. Data also tend to be insufficiently specific as well as too narrow in scope for the range of management decisions which continually must be made. Typically, administrators also find it difficult to integrate evaluation data into a feedback and planning loop which crosses organizational levels and decision areas and which would continue to inform and revitalize the educational process.

With the new information systems technologies, administrators can expect to have access to more complete and complex evaluation data which can be integrated into a feedback loop for planning and organizational decision making. The capacity to use multiple measures of organizational functioning for purposes of evaluation, and at low cost, is a very significant feature of the new technologies. They also will allow schools or districts to reach beyond their own situation-specific information bases in order to learn about model programs and compare student and staff performance with other sites. One of the most promising features of the new technology is the capacity to facilitate research at local, state and national levels that tests and evaluates the power of "best practice" models in highly diverse school settings or situations. This capability should arm administrators with potent tools for evaluating the work of organizational services and for improvement and accountability.

Again, the six information system elements and the eight POS/ SDCoRBE task areas have been considered here primarily to illustrate the point that learning to apply the new technologies to educational management practice is by far the more important and challenging administrator training imperative. It is more than simply learning about how to "run" the technology itself. Training content enabling administrators to apply the technology effectively ranges all the way from learning about the history and status of technology development to learning sophisticated techniques for applying the technology to day-to-day administrative tasks and analysis and manipulation of complex data. Illustrations of the kinds of knowledge and skills which fall between these two extreme points of a training continuum are stated or implied above. One final conclusion can be drawn from these discussions about training content. The new information systems technologies offer to administrators fresh and extraordinarily productive ways of thinking about and dealing with ongoing educational problems. Training would encourage them to accept the responsibility to use it for reshaping management practices and redefining management accountability.

Implementation of Training

Creating and implementing revised training programs for administrators which meet these needs is a difficult challenge. Extraordinary demands will be placed on our administrator training systems and on administrators as we seek, collectively, to understand the assumptions behind integrated information systems and how these can be "made real" by applying microcomputer and Utility technologies. The range of potential applications of these technologies to educational practice is enormous. Further, the interaction between new instructional practices and management practices made possible by the technology will be particularly dynamic and complex. Two key points are important to explore: (1) planning for implementation of training and (2) resources to support training.

1. **Planning**: Planning for implementation of training should take several important factors into account. The training effort necessary for the full promise of integrated information systems to be realized in our educational systems will be immense, requiring intensive involvement on the part of all those who have responsibility for training educational administrators. Virtually all practicing and administrators in training (as well as those responsible for administrator preparation programs) will need to receive some level of training in the new technologies and their potential applications.

For most educational administrators, this training will require a journey into a world of thought and technology totally new to them. Those few already familiar with microcomputers and the use of information utilities still will need to be trained in the particular technologies embedded in the new information systems, microcomputers and the Education Utility in order to use them intelligently.

Also, administrators each will have to invest tremendous amounts of time and energy in training for the new technologies and in applying them to new management practices. There is no question this process will be strenuous and will take some years to fully master. Some current and preservice administrators will find they have special talents for learning and applying the new technologies and will relish the opportunity for training and revitalization of practice. Others, who have difficulty with either the training itself or with the changes which will unfold in educational practice, may opt to leave the field.

The successful application of the new technologies may also tend to cause a number of educators who had not previously seen "administration" as an appropriate or desirable career choice to opt for administration after all. The entry of persons who might be expected to have different sets of skills and experiences into training programs would have an impact on the cadre of professionals trained at preservice and, eventually, inservice levels.

In light of such factors, it is evident that revised administrator training efforts will have a greater chance for success if they take into account at the outset the scope and complexity of the training task. Planning for delivery of this training should begin promptly and involve the several groups which have an interest and stake in the shape and content of administrator training.

At a minimum, such groups as the American Association of School

Administrators (AASA), the National Association of Secondary School Principals (NASSP), the National Association of Elementary School Principals (NAESP), the University Council for Educational Administration (UCEA), the National Conference of Professors of Educational Administration (NCPEA) and the Council of Chief State School Officers (CCSSO) should play a role in planning. Central planning tasks should involve determining how each such group can participate most effectively in training delivery and how to build an informed consensus among their constituencies for supporting and embracing administrator training in the new information systems technologies.

2. **Resources**: The availability of resources to support training will influence, particularly in the short term, our conception of the shape and goals of these training efforts. Until information systems, microcomputer and Education Utility concepts and applications are fully integrated into administrator training programs and into the professional lives of administrators, requisite training will tend to be additive, most likely in the form of special preservice or inservice "courses," seminars or workshops. These additive efforts will require substantial new resources.

However, as information systems concepts and technologies become more integrated into the world of educational administration and more a part of the practices of the field, training will become less additive and more an integral part of ongoing administrator preparation programs at all levels. At that point, allocation of existing resources to the training effort should have occurred and the need for new resources will have diminished.

Clearly, then training in the new technologies and their applications will tend to require very substantial additional resources for some period of time, until existing human and fiscal resources are reconfigured to include this new training as an integral part of administrator training efforts at inservice and preservice levels. But the equipment, personnel and other costs of supporting revised administrator training currently far exceeds the resource capability of local districts or institutions of higher education.

At a minimum, these costs should be supported at the state level. Support from the federal level and from the private sector should be pursued vigorously as well. The very strong potential for this training to better enable educational administrators to respond to the social mandate for more effective schools, and thus benefit society at large, makes these investments of public and private resources not only appropriate but imperative.

Administrators are very key people in the nation's educational system. If the Utility is to be widely and effectively used throughout the nation, administrators will need to be involved, enthusiastic and prepared. This Section of Chapter Five has offered suggestions as to the nature and scope of the training effort needed to assure that administrators take full advantage of the Utility.

Preparing Parents*

The system of education in the United States, and other countries throughout the world, is complicated in part by the number of participants involved. The ultimate success of the Education Utility requires that all participants be involved with and understand the Utility. Teachers certainly are key participants, as are school administrators. Learners are the reason for the whole system. There is another group vital to the successful operation of the Utility: parents.

For the most part, parents are comfortable delegating the bulk of the responsibility for their children's education to the schools, as long as the schools are using traditional techniques to accomplish traditional goals. Paper, pencils and textbooks are tools which today's parents know and are generally comfortable with, for these are the tools with which the parents themselves learned. The advent of calculators and their inclusion as a learning tool in the classroom, caused many parents to question the school's instructional decisions. Parents asked about the impact of this new tool on the quality of their children's education. Knowing arithmetic facts, and how to calculate them, said parents, was a top priority in basic education. Many parents were adamant about changing such a basic education priority.

Today, parents largely are unconcerned about the use of calculators in schools. They recognize them to be essentially positive tools, which have had little of the feared negative impact on the learning of mathematics. Calculators have become a *nonissue*. Other innovations of this kind have been introduced into the schools, and, for the most part, have become accepted as part of everyday school life.

Computers seem to represent the next generation of this now familiar cycle. While some of the concerns expressed are predictable in light of past cycles, there seem to be some different perceptions about computers. Many parents see them as more mysterious and potentially a much more powerful intervention in schools. They also

---

*This section, and the next, were contributed by Annette Paperello, Shoreham-Wading River Central School District, Shoreham, New York.

have more generic concerns about computers in society, worrying about what computers are doing, or will be doing, in their lives. Sherry Turkle's (1984) book, *The Second Self*, captures much of this ambiguity in perceptions about computers. Parents vaguely are aware of the changes instigated by computer technology and are not sure if all are positive. Thus, while responsible parents do not want their children to be left out of important educational improvements or to be unprepared for the future, they often are quite understandably anxious and concerned that computers in schools exert a positive influence on the quality of education available to their children.

As the Utility is introduced to schools and communities, parents will want to know: What is the Education Utility? What is the educational philosophy behind it? How will it improve their children's education and preparation for life? How can parents and families benefit from the Utility? What skills will parents need to have to benefit? Will the Utility help them help their children, or will the Utility alienate children from parents, and parents from the educational processes their children experience at school? Answers must be available.

The Education Utility will provide an opportunity for parents to become partners in the education of their children, while at the same time becoming learners themselves. It is vital that parents believe in the value and values of the Utility, as much as school personnel. But these positive feelings by parents may not happen automatically. There are a number of avenues for achieving adequate preparation of and commitment from parents.

Because the ultimate success of the Utility depends greatly on parents, they must become active participants in all phases of the introduction and operation of the Utility in a local community. Parents ought to be part of the decision-making process which elects to subscribe to the services offered by the Utility. When various needs assessments concerning the Utility are conducted, parents ought to be included and their ideas evaluated. Parents need to be given frequent feedback about both successes and shortcomings of the implementation of the Utility in the local school system.

Parents must recognize that how the Utility is implemented will impact on its success. For example, parents could assist in alleviating the person-hours needed to establish and coordinate each school's local resources on the Utility system by volunteering to catalogue existing school resources that ought to be entered into the system. Until a keyboarding program for students is initiated and operating, parents could help students enter their work into the system, thus minimizing the amount of time students spend trying to type their first drafts of papers and other projects. This kind of parental involvement with the Utility not only supports the local educators' efforts to make the Utility operational but also helps parents understand how the Utility works and begins to establish parents as genuine working partners in their children's learning.

Commitment from parents also can be achieved by providing them with access to needed services, through the Utility. The essential advantage of the Utility, from the point of view of a community member, is its potential for virtually unlimited and instant access to information, training, retraining and social interaction. Through the Utility, schools can function as electronic townhalls. Homes with computer modems can gain access to hotlines that list local employment opportunities, available babysitters (and their qualifications), community events, stock market reports or other similar information. If parents pay a fee to the school for these services, they will aid the financial needs of the school. The school, in short, becomes the kind of community resource center described in Chapter Three. With the school as hub, the entire community can become involved in the flow of general information and educational activity.

These services, and this kind of parental involvement with the schools and the learning of children, is rather idyllic. The scenario is quite feasible, however, given the characteristics of the Utility. But as is true with teachers and administrators, the power of the Utility may be limited if parents do not know *how* to use the technology. Therefore, it will be important for the school or other agency in the community to make training in the many aspects of Utility use available to parents. For example, many parents may wish to learn the basics of how to get in and out of the Utility. Other parents would attend workshops, sponsored by the school, on how to work with students, at home, to use the Utility to complete homework assignments. Parents may want to receive training in how best to communicate with the school, using the facilities of the Utility. Or parents may wish to engage in a lifelong program of continuing education through the Utility.

By making parents active and interested participants in the initiation of the Utility in a local school and keeping them involved, parental concerns will be addressed regularly. Parents will be able to comprehend the positive impact of the Utility on their children and in their own lives and become partners in the education process. The community gains from the vitality of a population busy about the task of learning. And the Education Utility exists in a positive environment where its promise can be translated into realities.

Preparing Learners

The essential responsibility of schools is to prepare students for their future. The underlying goal of every school, therefore, is to create an environment in which students can develop the knowledge, skills and attitudes they will need. Into that environment of late have come computer technologies. Consequently, computer literacy is being heralded as one of the basic skills every person will need in the future to function as a citizen and a professional. The Education Utility represents a powerful manifestation of this new information economy. It is important that children and youth be prepared adequately to deal with the Education Utility because it is the learning environment, and thus the future, of these children that the Utility most seriously influences.

In thinking about computer systems in schools, one must ask: How will a computer aid learners to communicate and cooperate with each other? How does one establish an environment in which students constructively cooperate to solve problems? How does one train users to focus on discovering patterns of information and thereby develop higher order thinking skills through the use of computers? How can one train students to use the information contained in computers to generalize, analyze and synthesize? What does one put into the early training programs to foster continual growth in thinking and computer aptitude?

A number of recognized computer specialists have advocated access to computers for all children as soon as they accurately can strike the keys. These experts argue that access to computers enhances intellectual development in unique ways. The developers of the Utility also believe that unlimited access to computers for all students, at all age levels, will enable students to develop higher level and more creative thinking skills. Using learning technologies such as the Utility, the teacher becomes a facilitator of learning in the Rogerian sense, and the initiative for learning again rests with the student. Now, through the appropriate use of computers and telecommunication technologies, the focus of student learning can be on the formulation and understanding of relationships among ideas, rather than the static transmission of those ideas.

Given the general relationship that might exist between student and computer, how are students best prepared to take advantage of the intellectual and interactive possibilities offered by the Education Utility? It may be most effective to teach students how to use computers by integrating computer instruction into the ongoing curriculum of the student. That is, the most effective means of preparing students to use the Education Utility is to have them *use* the Utility as part of the planned instructional strategies for a given lesson or session. One of the weaknesses of previous attempts to use computer systems in education is that children have been "taught computers," often pulled away from learning in other parts of their curriculum. The Education Utility is a *tool* to help students learn skills and/or content and is not in itself something to be learned.

Having said that, however, it should be pointed out there are some things to be learned about the Utility itself that will make it easier for students to use it as a learning tool.

The first of these skills is keyboarding or typing. The hunt-and-peck method could seriously undermine a student's ability to communicate thoughts or to become involved in higher-order thinking. At the very least, by the fifth grade students need to be able to touch type at about 30 wpm. Students then will be able to concentrate on *learning* rather than the mechanics of communicating with the Utility system.

A second skill is learning the major commands for whatever word processing program the students will be using. Again, word processing is a basic tool for subsequent efforts by students to communicate their thinking. There may be a variety of ways to teach these commands to students and different degrees of understanding of commands, depending on age levels. What is critical is that students know word processing commands sufficiently to feel free to give creative expression to their thinking. Many writers have commented that word processing capabilities changed in important, positive ways how they go about the act of writing. The same observation might be made about students seeking to communicate their thinking.

Third, students need to know how to manipulate effectively the Utility itself. Students will need to be able to log in and out effortlessly. Once logged in, students must be able to gain easy access to the various programs and data bases available. Although the Utility itself is being designed to be very "user friendly," it is vital that all students receive adequate instruction in how to work the system.

While the more concrete skills, such as those listed above, are very important, there are more abstract skills which need to be delineated carefully and learned. The rationale of the Utility is that through using it efficiently and effectively, students will achieve higher level thinking, problem solving capabilities and constructive cooperation and communication with others. The Utility creates a *context* within which teachers can help achieve these goals. The Utility can, through its various programs and materials, present interesting intellectual problems for learners, and the teacher can help students address those problems. By enabling constant communication with teachers and with other students, the Utility supports a dynamic learning environment. The Utility, in short, should not create an environment that *isolates* students, but rather one in which cooperation is encouraged and rewarded.

As students use the Utility, they will want to know how to make increasingly sophisticated use of it. The school (and the Utility) must be prepared to respond. Students should not be forced into a position of having learned all there is to learn through the Utility. The natural drive and curiosity of learners will take them a long way, if artificial barriers are not put in the way. There are times when more formalized instruction will be needed to help learners accomplish new goals with the Utility. The Utility itself should provide some of those instructional packages, but teachers and others also may need to be ready to offer instruction in using the Utility for expanded purposes.

Initial and continuing preparation programs needed for teachers, administrators, parents and learners to develop facility with the Utility require a unique partnership among the various institutions and agencies currently offering training or preparation programs in education. As has been stressed throughout this chapter, training is vital to the successful use of the Utility by any and all of the participants in the learning society.

It is evident that most preparation programs currently offered in colleges and universities will need to be examined carefully and revised, if those programs are to prepare future educators to use the learning technologies represented by the Education Utility. It is also evident that revisions in teacher and administrator preparation programs in colleges and universities will require a commitment to faculty development programs for *professors* in higher education, who are largely responsible for training future educators. Few of these professors will themselves have the kind of preparation needed to teach the instructional and administrative skills necessary to function effectively in an environment which includes the Education Utility.

Just *how* all of this training might be undertaken is a complex issue. In Chapter Six, some suggestions for how to accomplish the task are made, as part of a broader discussion of how users of the Education Utility might be supported.

CHAPTER SIX

USER SUPPORT SYSTEMS

One of the most unique and important characteristics of the Education Utility is the commitment of the developers to provide a comprehensive network of support services for users. There has been no past attempt of this magnitude to carefully plan for an integrated technology application in American education. Too often, educators have found themselves in a "let the buyer beware" environment, where the *sale* of hardware systems has been all that mattered. As a consequence, educators often found themselves surrounded by quickly obsolescent hardware or other educational "solutions," without benefit of a support system that encouraged and assisted in integrating the technologies into teaching and learning strategies. Educators also became isolated in their newly purchased technology and, predictably, soon stopped using the technology altogether. There are growing fears that a similar phenomenon might occur with microcomputer technology.

There are a variety of reasons why technological innovations fail to achieve their initially imagined potentials. In some cases, the limitations are in the technology itself. In still other cases, as was argued in Chapter Five, teachers, administrators, learners and other key actors in the education system are not adequately prepared to integrate and use the technology. And in still other cases, technologies gather dust in closets because the *content* for them is not appropriately structured for the technology or, equally common, there simply is a *shortage* of enough quality material for it.

Mindful of the lessons of history, the creators of the Utility have given a great deal of thought to the development of a support system that will overcome some of the limitations apparent previously. Chapter Six discusses some possibilities:

1. A major research, development, and training center, the Academy of Learning Technologies, which might serve as a focal point for a wide range of services to support the continued development of the Utility, and to recognize individuals who make substantial contributions to education.

2. A network of demonstration centers to provide users (and potential users) with an opportunity to see the Utility in practice. These would also serve as centers of training for the Utility and as sites for experimentation and research.

3. Linkages with professional associations, research and development centers, and governmental bodies, to ensure that the Utility is integrated into the education system in meaningful ways and that the Utility benefits from ongoing research and evaluation.

Each of these components is described in greater detail in this chapter. At the time of this writing, they are *ideas being considered*; other possible approaches could well be pursued in lieu of, or in addition to these concepts.

The Academy of Learning Technologies

The conceptual cornerstone of the Education Utility user support system could be the Academy of Learning Technologies. The Academy could provide a national and international forum for the exploration of matters related to the uses of learning technologies, with particular emphasis on further understanding about how the Education Utility could be used most effectively. The Academy could provide Utility users with a source of both theoretical and practical ideas and serve to stimulate research, evaluation, development, and training activities that benefit all users of the Education Utility. It also could support any educator attempting to use learning technologies of any kind more effectively.

The Academy could engage in a variety of activities with educators throughout the world, including:

1. The Academy, working closely with individual educational researchers and research agencies, could sponsor and generally promote research activities related to technologies in general, but specifically to the concept, utilization, and effectiveness of

the Education Utility. In pursuing such research, the Academy could undertake activities that would contribute to future developments of the Utility itself, improve instructional practice in a variety of learning settings and explore important policy issues. These activities might include:

a) develop an exciting research agenda germane to the purposes and practices of the Utility and other technologies

b) establish strong linkages with existing research and development centers to conduct and promote joint research activities;

c) plan and convene conferences, workshops, etc., on research topics related to learning technologies;

d) serve as a clearinghouse (and establish linkages with existing clearinghouses) for information for researchers and users of the Utility; and

e) attract scholars to spend time at the Academy pursuing research projects and ideas.

2. The Academy would further assist Utility users and other educators in evaluating uses of the Utility by:

a) developing evaluation plans and strategies to assess the Utility;

b) working with AT&T/NIU to develop evaluation strategies and software programs, and make such programs available through the Utility distribution system;

c) working with groups and agencies to develop creative means of assessing and monitoring student achievement; and

d) providing evaluation training and technical assistance to interested users of the Utility and to those who will be the trainers.

3. The Academy would not likely engage in extensive software or program development. The Academy could, however, explore issues related to the development of new learning strategies and/or materials for use in conjunction with the Education Utility, as for example, the use of "expert systems." In pursuing this, the Academy would define needs for new learning strategies and materials; stimulate the development of new and needed educational programs; and, in general, develop new ideas about how the Utility and other technologies might be integrated more effectively into instruction. The Academy thus could serve as a major support for users of the Utility who are seeking advice about instructional strategies and program selection, and to developers of new educational materials, strategies and programs.

4. The Academy also could address issues of personnel development. As has been previously argued, the preparation of educators and learners to use the Utility effectively is fundamental to its overall success. The Academy itself would not offer extensive direct training but could aid personnel development by activities such as:

   a) Planning and offering "trainer of trainers" programs for key leaders in the sectors of the education system using the Utility, such as colleges of education involved in teacher training, professional associations which provide continuing education programs for members, directors of human resource development departments in business and industry, AT&T personnel, affiliate personnel, and others;

   b) Work with demonstration center personnel (see below) in developing continuing education programs at those centers;

   c) Study issues related to training educators and learners to use technologies such as the Utility; and

   d) Sponsor conferences and workshops on topics related to personnel training and development.

5. Another category of activities for the Academy could be the study of various policy questions raised in the implementation of the Education Utility or other technologies. The Academy might:

   a) Convene representatives from groups having a stake in education and in the use of the Utility, to delineate key policy issues raised by the Utility and develop an agenda for the study of those policy issues;

   b) Commission policy papers on selected topics, using those papers as stimuli for Academy discussions;

   c) Convene a regular policy studies seminar in the Academy, inviting outside guests to join the seminars; and

   d) Publish and disseminate regularly papers on various policy issues. These papers should stimulate a national dialogue on topics related to technology uses in education.

There could be two additional and very vital aspects to the work of the Academy. First, it might be envisioned as a major "think tank" on topics related to learning technologies. Consequently, the Academy could host a significant number of scholars/researchers for study at the Academy. The Academy itself could support a number of these scholars, for periods of time ranging from a few months to a year or more. Some scholars could study topics outlined by the Academy. Other scholars could be invited to pursue topics which *they* have proposed to the Academy. In addition to the scholars financially supported by the Academy, other individuals could be in residence for a time at the Academy, with their home institutions or companies supporting their stay. For example, the Academy would be attractive to higher education faculty members with sabbatical leaves. In these circumstances the Academy would provide office and support services. The Academy also would host visiting scholars from abroad. One purpose of the Academy, then, would be to create a community of scholars, from a variety of disciplines and institutions, to mutually explore issues of importance to understanding the future of learning technologies.

The Academy also could sponsor a program recognizing those individuals who have made outstanding contributions to improvements in the quality of education. The Academy could award the annual Taub prizes for Excellence in Education, to individuals whose contributions in research, development, or practice have enhanced significantly our understanding and/or practices of teaching and learning, with particular attention to the applications of technologies in education. These awards would parallel in importance and recognition similar awards in other areas of endeavor, such as the Pulitzer Prize or the Nobel Prize. The awards, made possible by contributions from the founder of the Education Utility, Jack Taub, would recognize the centrality of education to a workable and just society and the importance of those individuals committed to ever more effective and substantial educational systems, materials and practices. The awards would be made at a prestigious annual event, meant to both recognize recipients of the awards *and* to recognize the importance of education in society.

The Academy should occupy an attractive physical location, conducive to its creative activities. It would be viewed as a permanent commitment to the idea that those who use the Education Utility must have a continuing source of new ideas and support, and that those responsible for developing and managing the Education Utility also must have a source of new ideas for and reactions to the Utility. The Academy could serve as a critical bridge among all sectors of the education system and the corporations which manage and/or are involved with the Education Utility. The Academy, as envisioned, would become a crossroads of intellectual excitement and a source of ideas and encouragement for those wishing to improve educational practice with learning technologies. There is no comparable resource today. The Academy would be a forum for the advancement of understanding of the next generations of technological applications in education and the societal impacts of those changes.

Demonstration Centers

One of the most powerful ways to learn about a technology is to see it in action. To that end, a network of demonstration centers, called the Education Utility Demonstration Center Network, could be established throughout the nation (indeed, throughout the world), allowing those interested in the Utility to learn about its possibilities in a variety of educational settings, through direct observation.

General Purposes of the Demonstration Centers

While specific demonstration center purposes will differ from center to center, there are certain general ones the demonstration centers would be designed for, including:

1. Each demonstration center would provide opportunities to view how the Utility is, and can be, used with learners. Visitors to the center would view the direct instructional, as well as administrative, uses of the Utility. Visitors would be encouraged to work with the staff of the center to explore ways in which they might use the Utility. Demonstration centers would, in short, provide opportunities to see how the Utility works in practice, with real students, teachers, administrators and support personnel. It is one thing to read about a concept in the abstract, and quite another to see the concept working in a real setting.

2. Demonstration centers could carry out systematic experiments with different uses of the Utility, exploring the potentials of this and other learning technologies. Demonstration centers ought to be places where imaginative uses of the Utility are encouraged, where there is a desire to learn from failures as well as successes. Demonstration centers could provide opportunities to explore different instructional strategies, different approaches to software uses and development and unique uses of the Utility for administrative purposes. Demonstration centers ought to become lively exciting places where the quality of education could be improved for all. And visitors should share in that excitement. Furthermore, the demonstration centers would develop systematic *records* of these experiments for dissemination. Demonstration centers should, in short, be a source of field-based ideas for use of the Utility.

3. Each demonstration center could serve as a focal point for the conduct of research activities related to instructional technologies in general, and the Utility specifically. Students from higher education could conduct their research at the centers. Faculty members with research interests would be able to develop projects at these sites.

4. Demonstration centers could become active in developing and providing continuing education opportunities for educators, parents, community people, business people and others. These could be workshops, conferences or seminars on topics related to the uses of the Utility. This would contribute directly to the more general goal of providing an effective support for users of the Utility.

5. Implied in some of the purposes outlined above, but worth mentioning directly, is the role of the centers in software development and testing. That is, each center would create a development capacity, producing education materials uniquely for the Utility. In addition, of course, each center would try out and evaluate programming from other locations.

6. The demonstration centers could play a key role in helping to organize local and/or regional networks of Utility users. By creating a support system for users, the centers could put them in touch with each other on a regular basis to exchange ideas, solve problems, and the like.

With the Utility Demonstration Center Network in place, teachers and administrators would have places to go to see the Utility in action and to discover new ways of using the technology. Good research would be done at demonstration sites, thus expanding the general understanding of links among technology, teaching and learning. New ideas for education programming would be tried out in these centers.

Contexts for the Demonstration Centers

It is anticipated that many kinds of community, business and educational institutions will find the Utility an exciting tool or system to help accomplish the goals of those groups or institutions. To that end, demonstration centers might be established in the following kinds of contexts:

1. K-12 schools should be major users of the Utility. Consequently, a number of demonstration centers could be established for these institutions.

2. Higher education institutions will also be involved heavily with the Utility, both to train teachers and administrators and to deliver instruction to students in higher education. Some demonstration centers could be established in institutions of higher education.

3. Various agencies involved in continuing professional education in non-school settings could find the Utility an effective instructional tool. Demonstration centers could be developed to show

how the Utility might be used for continuing professional education of adults.

4. The military has an extensive educational system. Demonstration centers might be established in a variety of military education contexts.

5. It is expected that many uses can be made of the Utility in international settings. Demonstration centers could be set up at a number of international sites, enabling educators from throughout the world to discover how the Utility might be used for education in their nations.

One of the more exciting aspects of the demonstration center concept is that, while centers may well be established in each of the settings described above, they more likely would be set up cooperatively with two or more of these settings in partnership. For example, one demonstration center might be a partnership between a college of education and a school district. Another might combine an elementary or secondary school, a university and a business. State boards of education and regional education service centers might be partners in a demonstration center. Education partnerships are being talked about a great deal; the Education Utility could promote them in new and exciting ways. The demonstration centers not only could demonstrate the instructional and administrative potentials of the Utility but also the potential for joint ventures in the education system.

Focus of the Demonstration Centers

The Education Utility can be used for a number of purposes in any educational setting. Some educators will be interested in the full range of opportunities provided by the Utility, while other educators will have special interests in the applications of the Utility in certain content fields or administrative areas. The Utility Demonstration Center Network could attempt to provide demonstrations and other services directed at both the general and specific interests of educators.

The majority of demonstration centers might be of a general nature. That is, these centers would provide demonstrations of a range of uses of the Utility in a given educational setting, such as an elementary or secondary school. For example, a center established in a high school might include demonstrations of the use of the Utility to teach English, mathematics, social sciences, art and other content areas. In addition, such a center could demonstrate how school administrators might use the Utility to implement an achievement management information system, enveloping all students and subject fields.

Because most school districts subscribing to the Utility would want to use the technology broadly throughout their schools, the general applications demonstration centers would be extremely valuable sources of ideas and information. As stated throughout this book, one of the significant features of the Utility is its ability to integrate curricula and instructional strategies, including management strategies, heretofore virtually impossible to achieve.

A similar situation exists in higher education institutions. Colleges and universities are likely to want to use the Utility to deliver parts (or all) of certain undergraduate courses, enhance graduate student research projects or train certain professionals, such as teachers, or to serve as a research base for faculty. Again, a general applications demonstration center in higher education should help administrators and faculty in those institutions see a variety of ways the Utility would be useful to them.

Most of the demonstration centers would be for general applications. In addition, however, a limited number of target or topical demonstration centers might be established to demonstrate the use of the Utility for more specific purposes. For example, demonstration centers might be established to focus on one or more of the following areas:

1. Mathematics and science teaching
2. Arts and humanities teaching
3. Occupational/vocational preparation
4. Rural schools applications
5. Multicultural education applications
6. Global education programming
7. Administrative operations
8. Undergraduate teacher preparation

The intent of these topical centers would be to further develop specific uses of the Utility and to disseminate such findings to users with particular interest in such areas. Work done in the topical centers eventually would be integrated into the general applications centers.

The above list of topical centers is meant to be illustrative, not comprehensive. Careful thought would have to be given to which of these areas, or others, ought to be the focus of topical demonstration centers. The *concept* is what is important at this point. These topical demonstration centers would provide a very special and needed support services to users of the Utility.

Activities and Services

What would actually take place in a demonstration center and what kinds of services might these centers provide? The activities and the services would vary from center to center, depending on context and focus. There are, however, some general descriptive statements that might be made about center activities. (Note: each center eventually would have a detailed operational plan, setting forth goals, activities, and services to be provided by that center. It is anticipated that a catalogue or inventory of the focus and services available from each center would be developed and made available to any interested educator. Such a catalogue would be helpful to educators in deciding which demonstration centers to visit or contact.)

Activities. Among the activities that might be undertaken by each center:

1. The main activity of each center would be to *use* the Utility. Each center would *demonstrate* how the Utility could be used in practice. It is expected that each center would be busy all the time, as faculty, administrators, learners, community members and others get involved in many of the learning and management tasks made possible by the Utility. It is perhaps trite to observe that the main task of each demonstration center would be to use the Utility, but that is precisely their intent.

2. While using the Utility, each demonstration center would also be expected to *evaluate* the various uses of the Utility. What works? For whom? What are the difficulties encountered by users? What appear to be limitations in the system, and how can those limitations be overcome? Who learns what? What kinds of instructional strategies seem most suited to the Utility? How, in fact, do teachers and learners use the Utility? These questions, and countless others, should help frame the evaluation activity. The intent of these evaluations would be to begin to form a body of experimental knowledge about the uses of the Utility, to find patterns of usage that seem most effective and to better understand how individual learning styles can be accommodated by the Utility. Evaluation activities also form the substance of what must be *disseminated* about the Utility.

3. Evaluation activities address certain kinds of important questions. It also would be important that the demonstration centers serve as sites for educational *research* about technological applications in education. Such research should be directed at principles that over the long haul would influence program devel-

opment and instructional strategies. Investment in research is critical to the long range development of the Utility concept. It is expected that research on or about the Utility would be undertaken by a number of agencies and individuals; demonstration centers could well provide the sites for a broad range of research activities, conducted by a variety of people and agencies.

4. Demonstration centers also could be busy with *development* of new materials and alternative instructional strategies for classrooms or other settings, given the power and versatility of the Utility. Demonstration centers could be places to experiment, to try out new and different ideas. As a result, demonstration center staff might begin to develop teaching guides, useful to teachers (or administrators) who want to use the Utility in other settings.

5. *Communications* would be one of the major activities of these centers. The communications would flow among demonstration centers, between centers and other Utility locations, between the center staff and researchers and a host of other linkages. The centers would be in the business of information and education.

These are but a few of the activities for demonstration centers on a day-to-day basis. These centers would be active, busy places, where different activities would support their various missions and purposes. There would be excitement here, as people search out new opportunities for teaching and learning. The demonstration centers would exemplify the kind of social and intellectual environment we all hope for in a quality education setting.

Services provided by the centers. From all this activity at each center would come services for interested consumers. These might include:

1. Demonstrations. Those visiting the centers would be able to see the variety of uses to which the Utility could be put, which should make it easier to see how the Utility might be used at their institutions. Each center would make demonstrations available to interested parties, of course, but the real power of the centers would lie in their capacity to translate into reality the concepts or theories of the Utility, to show how the system works *in practice.*

2. Demonstration centers would make available to interested users lesson designs or teaching guides that outline specific instructional programs the center had found to work. For example: a

K-12 general applications center may have developed an effective sequence of instructional activities on a topic in American history. A guide might be developed (in print or in an electronic form, or both) that contains a detailed description of goals for the unit of study, instructional activities employed and a catalogue of the materials and/or databases found in the Utility that were used for the lesson or unit of study. In some respects, these guides would approximate teachers' manuals or curriculum guides but would also include an inventory of relevant data bases from the Utility that could be used.

3. Demonstration centers would make available a broad range of continuing professional education opportunities for interested individuals, or groups of individuals. These could take a variety of forms, such as half-day conferences, workshops, courses of study offered in conjunction with a higher education institution, or teleconferencing. Continuing professional education programs, on a variety of topics and packaged in a variety of ways, could prove to be one of the most effective services offered by the demonstration centers. These continuing education opportunities clearly would contribute to the support system for users of the Utility. Such opportunities would provide a chance for individual users to continuously encounter new ideas, new ways of using the Utility. The individual teacher need not be alone to deal with the technology; the demonstration centers could provide a central hub or link among users, thus providing users with both the sense and the reality of an ongoing support base.

4. In addition to providing opportunities for visitors to observe the Utility in action, demonstration centers would provide interested consumers with technical assistance and consultation. That is, the demonstration centers would serve as one link in a general information and technical assistance support network. Demonstration center staff would assist personnel in school districts considering subscribing to the Utility to develop realistic plans for it in those districts. Staff might consult with users on appropriate instructional strategies, administrative uses of the Utility, or how to generate revenues by selling excess capacity. The demonstration centers could thus become a source of information and troubleshooting for actual and potential users of the Utility in their areas.

5. Each demonstration center would develop a publications (print and electronic) program to share information about the Utility. For example, a particular demonstration center in higher edu-

cation might create a monograph series focused on a line of research with the Utility. Newsletters would be disseminated on a regular basis. Electronic bulletin boards and computer conferencing might be established on a regional basis to provide a means for ongoing communications among users. Again, these publications would provide an important element in an overall support system for users.

Individual demonstration centers would undoubtedly pioneer other kinds of services for interested parties. There is little question that the system of demonstration centers would become focal points for experimentation, research and evaluation, program development and dissemination of information. The demonstration centers could provide overall support for individuals and institutions using the Utility to improve the quality of education. Demonstration centers have in the past been exciting places in which to work and to observe. That tradition would continue, and indeed be enlarged, through the Utility Demonstration Center Network.

Linkages with Associations and Centers

An important component in the support system for users of the Education Utility involves establishing linkages or partnerships between AT&T/NIU and existing professional associations and research and development centers. The primary vehicle for pursuing these partnership arrangements might well be the Academy.

Most educators identify with one or more professional associations and tend to look for leadership and support from them. Similarly, educators often look to education research and development centers for ideas and strategies useful in improving education practice. Associations and organizations maintain a network among interested educators through conduits such as newsletters, journals, conferences, leadership seminars and the like. It is vital that key members of the professional associations and the staff of research and development centers play a role in shaping the direction of the Utility and in involving their support members. This section sets forth some ideas about how AT&T/NIU and the Academy of Learning Technologies might work with the associations and research organizations to effectively implement the Utility, and thus support users.

There are a number of functions professional associations could play in developing the Utility and supporting users:

Create awareness

One of the most valuable functions associations can perform is to make their constituency aware of the Education Utility. Associations tend to be organized around specific positions held by educators (e.g., school administrator), or around specific content areas (e.g., social studies or mathematics). They could increase awareness about the Utility among members through notices or articles in newsletters or journals, sessions at national and regional conferences, or direct mailings to members. Information from professional associations about the Utility and other learning technologies could increase greatly awareness of the Utility.

Stimulate program / software development

Associations could play a pivotal role in stimulating the development of programs/software for distribution via the Utility, and thus in supporting efforts of members to use the Utility. This might be achieved by the association:

- Conducting needs assessments among membership to determine areas in which members feel programs and/or software are needed;
- Describing innovative programs already developed which might be used as models for similar program development activities;
- Establishing a regular or electronic mailbox for the ongoing communication of ideas among members about software development projects and procedures; or
- Through newsletters and/or other channels of communication, informing members of the opportunities for developing software that could be distributed through the Utility.

Stimulate research activity

In a similar fashion, professional associations could stimulate a great deal of research about the Utility, as well as research *using* the Utility. Using existing communications channels, associations could:

- Publish the results of research studies on the Utility;
- Develop thematic conferences, or sessions of conferences, directed at research on or about the Utility;
- Sponsor small grant competitions, in cooperation with funding agencies, for research on Utility-related topics; or
- Publish monographs about the Utility as it is used in the kinds of settings represented by the association.

One of the most difficult objectives in educational research is to develop and pursue a sustained *program* of research, in which a variety of research problems, projects, or issues add up to something greater than the sum of the individual research projects. Professional associations could be instrumental in helping to define and then pursue, through their membership, programmatic research efforts related to the Utility as an example of technology in education. These prospects, together with the potential for systematically translating research into the improvement of educational practice, are exciting indeed and just might be possible with the Utility as the organizer.

Provide training for members in using the Utility

Professional associations could take a leading role in preparing and supporting their members in using the Utility effectively. Many professional associations have active programs of continuing professional education for members. The American Association of School Administrators, for example, sponsors a wide range of continuing education programs for school administrators. The American Educational Research Association sponsors training sessions prior to its annual meeting. The National University Continuing Education Association, through its regional affiliates, sponsors meetings on critical issues in continuing education. Virtually every professional association offers such continuing education activities to its members.

Associations could thus take the lead in offering continuing professional education about the uses of the Utility to its members, through specialized workshops, annual conference sessions, publications and other familiar channels and activities.

What would be particularly exciting and effective, of course, would be for professional associations to begin to use the Utility itself. The Utility could be used to train members in how to use the Utility; beyond that, however, the Utility could become a key means whereby members could gain access to other kinds of quality continuing education programs. One of the most obvious benefits would be the ability of the Utility to electronically link members of associations together in unique new ways. Such communication patterns usually turn out to be one of the best forms of continuing education!

Provide consultation and advice

Because the Utility would represent a new and complex concept, everyone associated with implementation of the Utility would be learning continuously about the system and needing feedback as to what works and what doesn't. Professional associations could be a very important source of such feedback and input, with association representatives:

- Serving on advisory boards to the leadership of the Utility;

- Serving on various ad hoc study groups sponsored by the Utility;

- Providing guidance in the selection of research thrusts and software development priorities; or

- Engaging in various evaluation programs related to the Utility.

This feedback into the management of the Utility system would reinforce *user* concerns and issues.

These, then, are some of the functions professional associations could perform in helping implement the Utility and supporting its users. Each of these functions could be spelled out in considerably more detail, of course, and undoubtedly others could be identified. Associations are vital components of the education system. They represent in-place communication networks and a rich body of experience that must be tapped if the Utility is to mature.

In somewhat of a similar vein, users of the Utility and other learning technologies ought to receive support for their efforts through more direct access to the work of existing research and development centers. The contributions research and development centers can make to a user support systems include: expanding the theoretical base for education practice; making available instructional programs that have been carefully designed and tested; helping educators develop their own inquiry skills; all of which can in turn be put to good advantage in implementing the Education Utility.

No company nor any technology can continue to improve unless a research and development commitment is made to continuously expand knowledge about the technology. The education system itself, through existing research and development centers and programs, provides a rich source of information for improving educational practice. Yet, our history in effectively using education research is spotty. It is possible, however, that the relationship between research and practice can be greatly strengthened under the general auspices of the Education Utility, because the Utility provides both a focus and a mechanism for encouraging good research and the *use* of research data. Certainly, existing research and development centers should be a strong element in the support system for those who use the Utility.

There exists, in many pockets in the education system, a pervasive feeling of both cynicism and fear regarding technology-based interventions. There is fear that there will be no system of support for the educator who wishes to use technologies in education.

The developers of the Education Utility have recognized the imperative to provide the individual teacher, administrator, parent and/or learner with a strong and obvious support base. For the individual educator, there must be a source of new ideas, a network of people with similar concerns and experience, if that educator is ever going to be able to use technology to improve the quality of education offered to children or adults. The awesome potential of the Education Utility either can be perceived as an incredible resource to be used, or a terrible threat. *How* educators view the Utility will depend on large measure on their assessment of the support they will have. The system proposed in this chapter is intended to argue that a strong support system must in fact exist, if the Utility is to be viewed as a powerful resource for teachers, parents and all learners alike.

CHAPTER SEVEN

THE EDUCATION UTILITY
IN OTHER SETTINGS

The first six chapters of this volume have focused primarily on the use of the Education Utility in elementary and secondary schools in the United States. The potential for the Utility in those schools is great, but the Utility's applications are not *limited* to elementary and secondary schooling. Indeed, the prospects for creative and meaningful uses of the Education Utility are evident equally *outside* the boundaries of K-12 schooling, for much of the learning activity that occurs in this nation and, indeed, throughout the world, happens in places other than schools. This chapter contains an overview of ways in which the Utility might be used in other educational settings, for a variety of educational purposes. One of the most exciting aspects in the development of the Education Utility is that it might be instrumental in forging new educational partnerships in the education system. If conceived properly, these could bring enormous new strength to education efforts across contexts and populations.

This chapter contains an examination of possible uses of the Education Utility in:

1. Community educational services;
2. Vocational-career preparation and counseling;
3. Higher education applications;
4. Continuing professional education applications;
5. Corporate education and training applications; and
6. International education and exchanges.

It should be emphasized, as has been true throughout this volume, that the ideas presented are *illustrative* rather than definite. A magical part of any journey is the dreaming and speculating about what could happen. These concepts are meant to stir the imagination, to suggest ways the Education Utility indeed can contribute positively to the creation of an exciting learning society.

Community Educational Services

Previous chapters have contained references to the idea that schools with the Education Utility might become centers in the community for all kinds of information, education, and social services and activities. Following are more concrete ways the Utility could serve the education needs of a community:

1. **The Utility could serve as a community educational bulletin board** providing all community members with a source of information about educational opportunities and services in the community. Schools and other educational agencies could use this bulletin board for announcements to the public. And community members could add to the information available, ask questions about announcements, even register for courses electronically.

2. **The Utility could serve as as a link between individuals with needs for education services and providers of those services.** For example, someone from the community could indicate, through the Utility, that he/she was interested in learning more about a particular topic. Another citizen with expertise in that topic might respond and begin a dialogue. Or another individual in the community might contact a particular service agency that had announced through the Utility, a program on a certain topic. The Utility could provide for individual community members to get much more involved in both seeking out educational opportunities and in sharing their special interests or expertise. The networking possibilities are tremendous. One can envision a community where virtually everyone is actively involved in pursuing topics and activities of interest to them, drawing on the rich resources of the community.

3. **Programs in adult basic education or adult literacy could be developed and offered through the Utility**. It is difficult to obtain a precise accounting, but it is estimated that nearly 23 million adults in the United States are functionally illiterate. The Education Utility, housed in schools, libraries, and other public facilities in the community, and available from other locations by a local telephone call, might prove to be an ideal delivery system for at least some educational

programs aimed at reducing adult illiteracy. Many adult illiterates are embarrassed to admit they cannot read or do simple math. The Utility could present high quality literacy training, perhaps combined with video and other technological programs, that would permit adults to become literate in a private and personal manner. The Education Utility could be used as part of some of the successful volunteer literacy programs, such as those sponsored by Literacy Volunteers of America.

4. **The Utility might be an effective community resource in providing parent education programs**. Programs could cover topics such as helping parents to work more effectively with their children to complete homework, providing educational programs on drug and substance abuse, providing general information on child rearing or providing a network for parents with common problems or concerns.

5. **The Utility could be used to transmit other kinds of vital information for families, such as health care information**. An example of this might be educational programs and information produced by the National Cancer Institute on prevention of cancer.

6. **The Utility could be used as an educational conferencing tool in a local community**. For example, many people in a community might be interested in an opportunity to participate in a network conference with the presidents of the American Federation of Teachers and the National Education Association, discussing critical issues facing teachers. Or an educational conference might be held on controversial issues such as tuition tax credits, or the voucher system, involving key leaders in these areas. One can imagine an endless variety of such conferences and topics, aimed at actively involving the community in dialogues about important public issues.

7. **The Utility might become the source for many community members to continue learning what would be impossible, or very difficult, without the Utility**. For those with terminals in their home, this system especially would be convenient. For those without home terminals, local schools and libraries could be equipped with the Utility and make it available to all. In time, hundreds of quality programs of study should be available to adults who wish to continue learning. Of course, adults should be encouraged to put together their own learning programs, using the resources available in the Utility. But attention should also be given to creating well-designed, adult-oriented instructional programs for those who learn best within a structured format. Once again, the potential is enormous, particularly when one considers the opportunities adults will have through the Utility to develop networks with people all over the world.

Vocational/Career Preparation

The Utility might also prove to be a powerful vehicle for delivering vocational and career preparation and/or counseling. The considerable literature on the character of work contains a great deal of discussion of changes in the nature of jobs and the increasing need for individuals to make lifelong adjustment. Choosing and subsequently preparing for a career are not as simple as they once were. Cornish (1983) captured some of the tone found in the literature on work:

> Choosing a career has never been as difficult as it is today. There are far more occupations than ever before, with new ones springing up every day, and the older occupations are changing radically. Add to that the fact that people are living longer and adopting new lifestyles, and it's no wonder that the notion of a lifelong commitment to a single career now seems a trifle quaint. A dentist wakes up one morning, decides he never wants to look into another mouth, and enrolls in a computer course. An actress decides that the theater no longer turns her on and joins a real estate firm. A plumber uses an inheritance to buy a restaurant and try his skills as a cook. (p.5)

While there is some debate over the proper role of the schools in providing vocational or career preparation, most agree the schools *should* provide career preparation or, at the very least, career counseling. The Utility could be very useful as a means of delivering career/vocational materials or counseling to young people, perhaps in many of the same ways that other curricular materials are presented. The focus of this section, however, is *not* the use of the Utility in *schools* to deliver vocational education, but rather on how the Utility might be used to promote or enhance vocational and career preparation *outside* elementary and secondary school settings, such as:

1. **The Utility could make available to interested adults a wealth of information about career options and requirements.** Well-designed programs could be tailored to meet the unique information needs or interests of *individual* adults using the system. These programs could be highly interactive and enable interested adults to have access to an enormous amount of information on jobs and careers. They could use the Utility as a kind of vocational counselor, or source of information in conjunction with a trained vocational counselor. The capacity of the Utility to add to the data base and revise materials in the Network Control Center on an ongoing basis makes the technology especially attractive in this environment of rapidly changing career paths.

2. **The Utility also could provide direct vocational instruction**. That is, programs could be developed to teach specific vocational skills or strategies at convenient times for adult learners. The instructional flexibility of the Utility makes it possible to design individualized programs that meet the needs or interests of most adults, and that utilize an array of resources heretofore unavailable in any single form. The possibilities for creative program developments in this area are immense and exciting.

3. **Central to both career counseling and direct instruction in vocational skills is individual assessment of career interests and abilities**. The Utility could be an effective means for individuals to assess their interests and abilities, with almost immediate access to the results. Various interest inventories, for example, might be made available to adults through the Utility, together with scoring and guide to interpretation of the results.

4. **The Utility especially might be powerful in involving adult learners in simulations of various workplace situations and career paths**. A learner could simulate the kind of work that gets done in a particular vocational setting to decide whether that vocation is attractive. Such simulated experiences should be very helpful to an individual who is uncertain about what kinds of careers to pursue and, as importantly, which careers *not* to pursue.

These are a very few examples of general ways in which the Utility might be used to promote quality vocational and career education opportunities. The significant point is that the Utility can be made available to adult learners in a number of settings (e.g., in schools after regular school hours, in community libraries, in the workplace) and can provide them with rich materials and instructional opportunities related to vocational development.

Key to the effectiveness of the Utility in this area, of course, is the quality of both the resources available and the management system that permits the learner to gain access to the resources in a way that makes good instructional sense. What would assure such quality is if those with interest and expertise in the area would design materials and strategies for the unique capabilities of the Utility.

It would be a shame if the Utility was used *only* as an electronic filing system of information about jobs. The Utility provides the opportunity for much more interesting and powerful approaches to career preparation. Surely, effective vocational preparation programs, both within and outside elementary and secondary schools, are vital to the productivity and competitiveness of the workforce, in this country and elsewhere. It is evident that elementary and secondary schools do not, nor *should* not, shoulder the exclusive responsibility for making sure all individuals are well prepared for their careers and jobs. Such preparation is by necessity going to occur generally outside elementary and secondary schools. What is needed is a system whereby this preparation is available to all learners, regardless of age or previous experience. The Utility could be an extremely important component of such a system. Creative people need to explore the power of the Utility for this important challenge.

Higher Education Applications

Higher or postsecondary education provides another arena for the Education Utility. Because higher education in the United States (and throughout the world) is so large and complex, it is difficult to capture in any comprehensive fashion the range of uses to which the Utility might be put. In some respects, the kinds of uses for the Utility in higher education roughly parallel those in elementary and secondary schools. However, there are some unique applications of the Education Utility to undergraduate and graduate programs:

1. **Professors may find it useful to include the resources and strategies of the Utility in teaching a given course**. For example: an English professor may wish to use the Utility to involve students in an interactive program to study particular writing passages, as well as in writing assignments using of the word processing tools of the Utility. A biology professor might use a simulation program from the Utility to illustrate a procedure very difficult to explain through traditional lecture methods. A psychology professor might assign students to use the Utility to gather certain research information through networks with students throughout the country.

2. **Entire independent study courses of study could be designed for individual higher education students**. Independent study is a time-honored instructional process in most higher education institutions. The Utility could provide incredibly rich independent learning experiences for students. Some of these would be designed by professors for students, but in other cases the Utility could provide the means for the individual student not only to pursue but actually to *create* his or her own study program, drawing on the wealth of resources available through the Utility.

3. **Using the Utility, institutions of higher education could offer high quality "distance teaching" courses, virtually anywhere in the world**. For example: a teacher education college might develop programming to supply its entire upper division baccalaureate program in elementary teacher education, via the Utility, to elementary and secondary teachers in a nation on the other side of the world,

where most teachers have little or no formal training in pedagogy. This degree program would permit the delivery of high quality course content but would also permit direct interchange, via electronic mail, between the professors involved in the degree program and participating teachers. Most importantly, the Utility would open up to the participating teachers all of the instructional resources available on the Utility. Higher education has a long history of providing such extended program services; the Utility represents a logical extension and solves some of the most pervasive problems associated with extended programs, such as the need to provide library resources or more effective interchanges between professors and students.

4. **Professors might find the Utility to be uniquely suited to promoting ongoing interchanges among professors with common interests.** The networking capabilities of the Utility could provide the means for scholars to collaborate more effectively and efficiently on research projects, writing activities and other academic work. In fact, the Utility could well become a major vehicle for disseminating scholarly work.

5. **Similarly, the Utility could greatly facilitate the gathering and sharing of certain kinds of research data.** This rather simple example illustrates the potential of the Utility as a *research* tool: a certain researcher wishes to collect survey data from a large number of seventh grade students, on a topic of interest to the researcher. The survey instrument could be entered into the Utility system, downloaded into as many schools as needed in the research study. The instrument could then be further distributed to the terminals of students, who are asked to respond to the items in the survey, using their terminals to reply. The responses made by each student are in turn forwarded electronically to the Network Control Center for aggregation and analysis by the researcher.

The implications of the Utility to promote educational research are tremendous. Yet careful attention must be given to the design of the software systems in the Utility so that this kind of data gathering can be enhanced, while at the same time assuring appropriate privacy and security protections for respondents.

6. **The presence of a Utility in an institution of higher education would be important not only for what information and services the Utility could bring to the administrators, faculty, and students of that institution, but also for what higher education personnel could bring to the Utility.** That is, the Utility would open up avenues for creativity on the part of users of the Utility. This would result not only in new programs and materials for distribution on the Utility but likely would result in rekindling the creativity of many faculty

members who may have become bored or disillusioned with their work and less than fully productive. Unfortunately, many professors suffer from loss of career vitality. The Utility could very well present an opportunity for some of them to begin a new and exciting phase in their careers, as they realize the instructional and research possibilities in the Utility. Many professors feel they do not have adequate or appropriate outlets for their ideas; the Utility could fuel new enthusiasm within the professoriate.

Again, these are very preliminary thoughts on the possibilities of the Utility at work in higher education. Hopefully, they suggest some broad parameters within which additional uses for the Utility in higher education might be developed. Just as the Utility has the potential to revolutionize the way teaching and learning occur in elementary and secondary school, so, to, does the Utility offer exciting opportunities for higher education. The sheer intellectual and creative energy in our nation's higher education institutions is awesome; the Utility may well provide a technological outlet for this talent. Higher education institutions play key roles in creating the Learning Society; the Utility can encourage higher education institutions to realize this role.

Continuing Professional Education*

Adult and continuing education has become a widespread and prominent activity in this country. For example, the housewife participates in a short course on home management offered by a university extension office. The business executive studies cost containment in a seminar offered by a professional association. The soon-to-retire worker is enrolled in a pre-retirement workshop provided by his/her employer. The unemployed worker is enrolled in a displaced worker training program offered by a community college. The retiree participates in a voluntary study group on the topic of managing personal finances offered by a local bank. Literally millions of adults are actively pursuing systematic learning and study activities in different settings, sponsored by a variety of institutions or groups. And literally billions of dollars are being spent each year to support these activities.

There are numerous reasons why adult and continuing education has become so extensive. The most fundamental are that adults participate in response to a personal need or to expectations held for

---

* This section on continuing education applications was contributed by Arden D. Groteleuschen, President, Grotelueschen Associates, Inc.

them by others. This need may be reflected in the desire to keep abreast of rapidly changing knowledge and information. It may be reflected in the desire to keep informed of societal changes — economic, social and political circumstances that affect their lives. It may be to enhance the quality of their personal well-being. The significance of such participation in adult and continuing education is not only fundamentally important for the adults themselves, but also for society and its institutions; adult participation in education activities forms the backbone of a strong learning society.

As our society increases in complexity and as the population becomes more adult-centered, the challenge of maintaining and developing society's human resources is a continuing and ever increasing challenge. Where should one then focus educational efforts? What should receive priority? Assuming that the Education Utility will be systematically used to address some aspects of adult and continuing education, but acknowledging that the Utility at the outset cannot respond to the entire adult and continuing education challenge, where shall the focus be? The remainder of this section will analyze possibilities and give examples of how the services of the Education Utility might be applied in adult and continuing professional education.

Appropriate initial programs involving the Utility would have to be determined after taking several factors into consideration. Targeted efforts might best be achieved if they were directed toward a potential clientele that:

1. Has a current high rate of participation in continuing education and has the prospect of increased participation;
2. Is a proportionally increasing segment in today's adult labor force;
3. Has the financial capacity to fund and sustain an education and information utility;
4. Is relatively socialized in the uses of modern technology;
5. Has an institutionalized setting in which a variety of potential learners work or are being served;
6. Relies heavily on providing services and using and generating information; and
7. Is critical to the general welfare of individuals, communities and the society.

If these criteria are examined carefully, one might conclude that professionals in our society may be an appropriate clientele for using the Education Utility. Proportionally to other adults, professionals have the highest participation rate in continuing education. They also are projected to increase their representation in the labor force from 4 percent in 1900 to 25 percent in the year 2000. Among the professionals in the society, healthcare professionals (e.g., physician, dentist, pharmacist, nurse) may well be a high priority group to focus on as an initial Utility group for continuing professional education. And, the criteria listed above suggest that the primary setting for the continuing professional education of healthcare personnel is the community hospital or healthcare facility.

Eventually, the Utility should provide education and information resources to many kinds of professional groups. However, as a way of illustrating how the Utility might be applied in one particular continuing professional education context, namely, in hospital settings to meet the continuing education needs of healthcare professionals, the following examples are offered:

1. **Most pharmacists today have some affiliation with a healthcare facility**. Having the Utility located in a facility such as a hospital might have numerous advantages. One is the potential access of users to medical and pharmaceutical information. The Utility could serve as a central clearinghouse on drug information. For example, information regarding clinical trials on drugs could be readily accessible through Utility services. Also, current information on drug interactions could be immediately accessed. Having available critical information about drugs, the Utility could offer prescriptive statements to pharmacists so that they could advise clients about their drug prescriptions.

2. **Much of patient management and treatment involves communicating information to the patient**. Frequently the information can be conveyed to the patient using television monitors or some other technological device. The communication capability of the Utility not only allows the patient to receive pertinent information, but the Utility can assist the patient with prescribed compliance and the monitoring of patient compliance.

3. **Even though the hospital is the primary workplace in which continuing education for healthcare professionals occurs**, considerable continuing professional education also occurs at regional and national levels. Information about scheduled events in a profession typically are mailed directly to professionals or printed in association sponsored journals. The problems of gathering and maintaining information about programs is extremely difficult and often inefficient because there is a reliance on printed, mailed material. Having information about continuing education programs displayed by the Utility not only would improve the accuracy and currency of adver-

tising efforts, but would be less difficult to administer. Providers would only have to interact with the Utility to provide information about sponsored events. Potential participants could access the information in the hospital workplace.

4. **In a manufacturing-oriented society, product warranty provides assurance to the public that product standards are observed**. In a service oriented society the quality of professional services is assured by professional licensure and certification. The trend (albeit not without considerable controversy) appears to be toward the expansion of licensure, certification, and recertification processes, both within professions and across professions. The capability of the Utility to administer computer adaptive testing to professionals in hospital sites is a likely prospect. Current professional knowledge could be effectively and efficiently assessed as well as professionals' capacity to think about practice-based problems using pertinent professional knowledge resources.

5. **Within communities the delivery of healthcare is in transition**. Hospital facilities, in many instances, serve as the hub of healthcare delivery. Extending from the hospital (and sometimes independent of the hospital) are services provided in ambulatory centers, nursing homes, physician group clinics, wellness centers and even homes. With this constellation of services, access and communication of information are vital for the satisfactory delivery of medical services. To illustrate, through the Utility, a hospital could serve as an information depository, so that outreach facilities could get specific patient information about blood tests, pathological analyses, patient histories, drug interactions, etc. Furthermore, the Utility could provide access to general scientific and clinical information. The hospital, using the capabilities of the Utility, thus would serve as a centralized medical information and knowledge resource for the community.

6. **With the trend toward establishing major healthcare consortia or alliances among different healthcare systems** (e.g., Allied Health Association, Voluntary Hospitals of America) and the extension of corporate hospital systems (e.g., Hospital Corporation of America, Humana), the use of the Utility as a partially dedicated delivery system for healthcare continuing education might be desirable. In addition, national healthcare networks are increasingly utilizing telecommunication techniques to share corporate information — financial condition, strategic plans, policy guidelines, marketing strategies — with its member systems. The ability of the Utility to transmit confidential information and to provide access to public information and knowledge is important to large hospital systems.

7. A final example is that the Utility could provide directly, to the public, information about a variety of well-being and care, fitness concerns. This "how to" and "what to do" information can be conveyed to workplaces and homes as a public service of a healthcare institution. In some sense, it can be regarded as a broader technological application of the kind of information that Dr. Benjamin Spock gave an earlier generation of parents through the printed media.

Providing an information Utility system for use by professionals in community healthcare settings presents an important opportunity and challenge for the Education Utility. Hospital settings, like other educational settings, are primary service facilities to our society. No community or region is excluded from medical or educational services. If the services of the Education Utility can be successfully demonstrated in selected sites, then the prospect for revolutionizing certain elements of society's ability to deliver healthcare information and knowledge resources will be enhanced greatly.

One can envision the Utility offering similar kinds of education and informative services to virtually *all* professions, such as accountants, lawyers, business administrators, real estate brokers, bankers, etc. All of the capabilities of the Utility that are so compelling for use by elementary and secondary schools are equally as attractive for continuing professional education: updated information resources; networking capacities; interactive instructional materials; etc. Imaginative uses of the Utility in continuing professional education will greatly improve the quality of what is made available to professionals.

Corporate Education and Training

Continuing professional education, as outlined above, is closely related to the broader notion of lifelong learning. Another sector of the education system that embodies the idea of lifelong learning is the so-called *corporate classroom*, the variety of education and training activities undertaken by the nation's businesses and industries, as well as the military system.

Eurich (1985) began her report on corporate classrooms with this introductory paragraph:

> Education and training within large private sector corporations of the United States have become a booming industry. Millions of adults, as employees, pass through corporate classrooms every year; and, an uncountable number more are given what is generally called on-the-job training. America's workers and managers have been going back to school for a long time, but in the last decade

their numbers have increased, the variety of subjects they study
has broadened and, most strikingly, America's business has become
its own educational provider. (p.1)

Eurich attempts to document the size and scope of corporate
investment in education and training. While the precise numbers are
difficult to delineate, by even the most conservative estimate it is
evident that education and training in the corporate sector are a very
big business indeed. Why corporations are investing such vast sums
in education and training is an interesting question. Eurich argues
that there are three basic reasons: compensatory education is needed
on both basic and advanced professional levels, company-oriented
education is vital for survival and recruitment, and employee benefits
are enhanced by educational opportunities.

A comprehensive review of the literature on corporate education
and training endeavors is beyond the scope of this chapter. However,
it may be sufficient to point out that numerous kinds of corporate
education and training programs exist. Some corporations offer their
own graduate degrees. Others provide specific skill-building workshops and training courses. Other corporations sponsor art exhibits
for employees, while still others have developed health promotion
and fitness education programs for employees. There are, in short,
a large number of organizational and pedagogical approaches to
education and training being used in the corporate classrooms
throughout America.

Given this enormous education effort taking place, how might the
Education Utility enhance corporate education and training? This
question could easily constitute the subject matter for a separate (and
extensive) book, for the possibilities of using the Utility in the
corporate education marketplace are numerous. However, a few
concrete ideas on the topic might stimulate the imagination of
corporate educators:

1. **Because of its ability to individualize educational programs,
the Utility might be a powerful delivery system for making basic
or remedial education available to workers in the workplace.** One
could imagine a Utility being set up in a factory and workers given
time to go to the Utility facility for basic literacy programs. Workers
thus could gain basic skills on their own terms, without risk of
embarrassment that sometimes accompanies studying in formal classroom settings.

2. **Similarly, the Education Utility could offer the opportunity
for employees to gain advanced technical skills in their particular
areas.** The interactive nature of the Utility would permit the devel-

opment of highly sophisticated educational programming aimed at teaching a wide range of skills. Again, one of the major advantages of the Utility will be that these quality skills training programs can be made available to employees *when* they need the skills. Individualization of skills training programs would be a substantial plus for corporate training efforts.

3. **New product information could be transmitted effectively and efficiently to corporate employees needing such information, wherever those employees might happen to be.** The Utility will permit security of new product information, limiting access only to those who need and should have the information. Furthermore, this information could be presented in fresh and interesting ways to employees, as the Utility makes possible a host of presentation modes. Employees could also interact with each other, through the Utility, to raise questions about new products.

4. **Many corporations are providing opportunities for their employees to study topics or areas not directly related to the employee's specific work responsibilities.** The value of the broadly educated employee is being recognized by more and more corporations. The Utility could make available to employees a great selection of adult learning courses to study, on a host of topics, that would result in a kind of learning society within the workplace.

5. **The Utility could provide effective instruction for employees who are changing jobs within a corporation, or moving from one corporation to another, and who have to learn a new set of skills.** Carefully designed programs on the Utility would be invaluable to orient new employees to the requirements of a particular job setting.

Numerous other examples of the use of the Utility in corporate education and training centers certainly could be described, but the underlying point to be made here is that the Utility's unique characteristics can be used in as powerful ways in the corporate education sector as in higher education or elementary and secondary education. The capacity to individualize educational programs, for example, is of great significance in the corporate training world. So, too, the Utility's networking capacity is of great importance in education and training. The Utility in the elementary and secondary sector opens up the world's information resources to young people; the Utility can open up for adult employees of corporations another world of information resources. The capacity to move information from a central center to a specific location, for subsequent use by learners there, has tremendous implications for corporate education and training. And the capacity of the Utility to make available educational programs that go well beyond the interest level and sheer instructional power of most current offerings opens the doors to vast new approaches to education and training in the corporate sector. The Utility is, in short, a dramatic new tool for enhancing the quality and quantity of education and training made available to employees by employers. The results should be evident in increased productivity, a better competitive edge for American business in the world economy, and increased job satisfaction for employees.

One additional observation by Eurich (1985):

> Large corporations, and particularly those on the high-tech front, are pouring time and money into keeping their personnel abreast of developments or, better yet, ahead. Their classrooms provide learning for the millions of adults who will change jobs or tasks four to five times in their work lives. Hence, any view of educational opportunities for adults in our society that does not include the corporate educational system is missing a major sector where countless numbers are learning. (p.22)

If the commitment to developing a true learning society is to be carried out, there is no question but what careful attention must be paid to the system of education and training in the military and corporate sectors. The overall plans for the Education Utility should include its role in the corporate education system. And not so incidentally, the Utility provides an extraordinary opportunity for building the kinds of relationships among corporations, elementary and secondary education institutions and institutions of higher education that are needed to establish the learning society. If each of these sectors uses the Utility, and if they are linked together *by* the Utility, mutually beneficial relationships just might happen.

International Education Applications

One of the most exciting applications of the Education Utility is in the international arena. Because of the telecommunications capacities of the Utility, it is now feasible to think of a global network for education and information exchanges. There is a growing realization that all of us live in a world where distances, both geographic and cultural, must be thought about differently. Our technology has made individual or national isolation virtually impossible; it is time we begin to use our technologies to capitalize on our interdependence.

The Education Utility could play a very vital role in attempts to make international education activities more possible and more beneficial. For example:

1. **At the most basic level, the Education Utility provides a**

mechanism for information resources to be made available to virtually everyone, anywhere. The implications of this are staggering. It means that no individual will have to be denied access to the world's information base simply by virtue of where the person is born or resides. Theoretically, given the Utility, the child in Kabul, in Lusaka, or in Chicago should be able to learn by having access to the same amount and kinds of education resources. The teacher in Jakarta and the teacher in Libreville will have access to as many teaching resources as the teacher in San Diego. There are, to be sure, a substantial number of political and cultural issues imbedded in this discussion. Some nations may restrict the kinds of information individuals can obtain. There is a danger that forms of cultural imperialism could develop, depending on who controls what information is available on the Utility system. There are language issues to be addressed, although it should be pointed out that the Utility will be able to deliver educational resources in whatever languages are necessary.

Making available these kinds of information and education resources throughout the world is no small matter. It is interesting to talk with individual students from abroad who come to study in American higher education institutions. A substantial number are preparing to return to their home countries to be teachers at various levels in the education system of their country. One of the most devastating problems faced by many international students is that, once they return to teach in their home country, they do not have the instructional resources they need. The Utility could change that. The Utility offers the informational resources support someone in another country needs to provide quality education experiences to the people in that country.

2. **Through the Utility, various kinds of preparation and training programs could be made available to interested learners in nations throughout the world.** For example: it would be possible to develop for delivery via the Utility a program of study designed to prepare nurse practitioners. Such a training program might be extremely valuable in nations where health care delivery systems need major strengthening. Individuals in those nations could receive high quality training in their own country, via the Utility. Similar kinds of programs could be developed in many vocational and/or professional areas. Not only could the Utility be used to deliver high quality course materials, and the necessary support information resources, but the Utility also could be used to provide a network for communications among learners in a given nation and specialists in a given topic area

from around the world. This electronic and ongoing technical assistance capacity makes the Utility unique. Too often, technical assistance consists of an expert traveling to a country, staying a very short time, imparting some knowledge or skills training, then departing, leaving the residents of the nation without a source of continuing support. The Utility provides a mechanism for continuing technical support.

3. **The Utility also allows a variety of educational programs to be made available to schools or other educational settings throughout the world.** In some cases, having access to information is in and of itself all that a teacher or administrator in a school in another country might want from the Utility. In other cases, however, teachers and administrators might want entire *programs* of study available for their schools. These programs could be downloaded to the computer of a school, in, for example, Penang, Malaysia. The teachers in that school could preview a particular program and determine how or if it would fit into the curriculum of the school. If the fit is a good one, the program can be used. It not, the teacher could consider other programs or *request* a certain kind of educational program.

This use of the Utility is essentially the same as schools in the United States will put the Utility. The significant point here, of course, is that these programs *also* can be made available to teachers and learners throughout the world.

4. **The Utility provides an opportunity for enriching its information by adding to its resource base materials and ideas developed in other nations**. That is, the Utility becomes not just a conduit for transmitting materials and ideas developed in the United States to people in other countries but also permits, and indeed encourages, a two-way exchange of information. American teachers might be able to learn valuable lessons in instruction from their counterparts in schools throughout the world. Certainly, the curricula offered in schools in the United States would benefit from an infusion of perspectives and materials from different places in the world. There is a tendency toward provincialism in many, if not most, American schools. The Utility, used to promote international or comparative education, could help change that.

5. **One of the most powerful educational possibilities of the Utility is the opportunity to create networks around the world.** An individual learner in International Falls, Minnesota, would be able to establish an ongoing dialogue, via electronic mail, with another learner in London, or Delhi, or Caracas. Out of this exchange would come a better understanding, by all parties, of different societies and hopefully, greater tolerance of differences among the world's peoples. A class of students in Selma, Alabama, could exchange essays with a

class of students in Montreal. Teachers in the United States could compare instructional strategies with teachers in Sweden. School administrators throughout the world could share ideas with their colleagues in ways not feasible without the Utility. Curriculum materials can be exchanged. Good ideas can be exchanged. And not insignificantly, goodwill can be exchanged.

Networks of peoples, cutting across national lines, have been established in the past. What the Utility brings is the opportunity for those exchanges to be carried out much more efficiently, and with less time consumed in *waiting* for replies and responses. The Utility can create a sense among those in the network of a "real time" connection, a more living and dynamic interchange.

6. **The Utility might also be used to promote and support mutual research and development projects across national lines**. Researchers in two or more countries could collaborate on research projects, using the Utility both as a data gathering tool and as a communications tool for the researchers. Manuscripts can be exchanged easily making joint writing projects more feasible and dynamic. Data analyses can be carried out more effectively, as researchers, using the Utility, can be looking simultaneously at certain data banks and jointly interpreting what they see.

It is never easy to carry out international research activities. Most often, these activities run into trouble because of elementary communications and distance problems. The Utility can help solve some of those communications problems. The time between interchanges can be greatly shortened. While logistical issues are usually only a small part of collaborative research activities, those logistics sometimes make or break an important research study.

7. **The Utility could also be instrumental in helping certain international professional associations carry out their work**. One example might be useful. The Pacific Science Association (PSA) is a 50+ member nation association, designed to promote the exchange of scientific, technical and cultural information among the member nations. The group holds a world congress every four years and an inter-congress midway between the world congresses. The PSA has been in existence for a number of years and has succeeded in promoting important exchanges.

Effective communications, however, have been difficult within the Pacific Science Association. The Utility could help in this area. If member nations were able to link individuals in each country with colleagues working in similar scientific areas in other countries, under the auspices of the PSA, communications would be enhanced, and the mission of the PSA more effectively undertaken. Exchanges of papers and other scientific activities could be made more efficient. Scientists could collaborate on research projects, using data bases available through the Utility. The possibilities are exciting.

It is probably not hyperbole to suggest that the Education Utility, used correctly in international settings, could very well play a critical role in promoting international peace and understanding. To the extent that individual citizens have a better understanding of their fellow world citizens, world peace is made more possible. To the extent that an *International* Learning Society will promote greater world understanding, the Utility promises positive influences on the very shape of the future world. It will be important for the Education Utility to be used for international education activities. The issues of equity, particularly those concerning who will have access to the Utility, may be raised to an international level: will the Utility be used to promote better education for *all* people, or only the rich? The question needs to be addressed.

The characteristics of the Education Utility make it useful in a variety of educational settings, in addition to elementary and secondary schools. Because the Utility is designed to be user-driven, the system can be flexibly used wherever educational activities are undertaken. In this chapter, a few suggestions have been made concerning how the Utility might be used in higher education, corporate education, continuing professional education, international education, and, in general, in any agency where education occurs. In addition, the role of the Utility in promoting vocational/career preparation, and as a general community educational resource, has been explored. Clearly, these ideas are in no way exhaustive, but rather suggestive of what might be done with the Utility to promote quality learning in a variety of settings.

Key to the successful use of the Utility in any educational setting will be the willingness of creative people to imagine new and exciting uses of the Utility in a given educational setting and then to put those ideas to work. The real uniqueness of the Education Utility as an educational tool lies in its almost infinite flexibility for the user. Educators need to decide how to make this tool work for them, and for society.

CHAPTER EIGHT

THE JOURNEY CONTINUES

This chapter is written in the first person because I want to provide some brief concluding remarks about the Education Utility from my personal perspective, as a person who has been an educator for some time. Quite frankly, the *concept* of the Education Utility is as powerful an idea as I have ever seen. The potential seems tremendous, but the pitfalls along the way also are significant. In this chapter, I share a few thoughts about both potentials and pitfalls.

The idea of opening the world's information resources to every individual, no matter who they are or where they might be, is mind-boggling. To be sure, not everyone will take advantage of this access to information, but that possibility should not lesson our enthusiasm. We constantly are reminded that we live in a time of a great knowledge explosion, that our future well-being depends to an increasing extent on our ability to acquire and understand new knowledge, and that, as Harlan Cleveland observed in the quote which began Chapter One of this book, people who do not "fine-tune their knowledge and their insights, will be left in the jetstream of history by those who do." At the same time, however, we as a society or an education system have not found feasible ways of helping *individual people* gain this new knowledge on a systematic basis. Of course, there always have been individuals who have found ways to stay abreast of the information explosion. Unfortunately, it does not appear that our nation's schools have mastered the art (or science) of providing individualized, infor-mation-rich programs of study for young people. In fact, too many of our young people leave our schools both with inadequate knowledge *and* a lack of desire to continue learning.

I believe the Utility represents a way to change this picture. The Utility, properly executed, makes it possible to deliver individually tailored, information-rich programs of study, through highly motivating instructional strategies, at a cost we can live with. We've simply not had such a tool before. There is tremendous potential here for a major change in the way teaching and learning takes place in this country and around the world.

These changes in teaching and learning strategies could produce very positive "ripple" effects as well. For example, I believe teachers who use the Utility will be renewed as teachers. We face grave problems within the teaching profession. There is considerable demoralization, burnout, fatigue, discouragement. Many of the best teachers are leaving the profession. The Utility could reverse this trend. Teachers could once again get excited, or stay excited, about teaching. The Utility could break down the barriers of isolation, reduce the lack of adequate instructional resources and transform bored and disruptive students into excited learners. The human drama and excitement of learning could be found again, and then teaching will be what it ought always to be: the most stimulating and rewarding of professions. From what I know of the Utility, and from how I've seen others react to the concept, I think these possibilities are more than just wishful thinking; I think the possibilities will become realities, if the Utility's implementation remains true to its design.

Furthermore, the potential of the Utility as the cornerstone of a lifelong learning society is awesome. One can envision a society in which adults freely and regularly explore new worlds of knowledge and information, even more so than today. Available statistics indicate that large numbers of adults pursue various kinds of learning projects. Given widespread availability of the Utility, I predict even more in the future will pursue their own learning activities. The quality of such activities could be improved, as imaginative programs and more information resources are available through the Utility. Furthermore, I expect the Utility will encourage more networking among adult learners, resulting in demands for even more Utility services for adults. While most of the energies of the developers of the Utility have been concentrated on elementary and secondary education, I would not be at all surprised if, over time, *adult* learners tend to use the Utility at least as much as K-12 learners. The Utility may, in fact, create a kind of seamless education system, blurring some of the current very sharp demarcations between elementary/secondary, higher and adult education activities. Learning may become genuinely "lifelong."

Another positive ripple effect of the Utility will be, in my judgment, a quantum increase in the amount and quality of educational software programs developed for use on the Utility system. The Utility provides a means for people who have good ideas for software programs to get those ideas into the education marketplace. The Utility makes it possible for an individual or institution, without an in-place marketing and distribution system behind them, to market and distribute products. If the products work, users will want them. If the product is *not* good, no one will choose to use it and the product will languish in the system. But what is important is that a producer at least has a *chance* of getting an audience with teachers and learners, through the Utility. Having a chance to market an educational product may be a sufficient stimulus to motivate many private developers to try their hand at educational materials development. I think it unlikely that large numbers of teacher suddenly will begin to turn out large quantities of new materials, although I hope some of that kind of development work occurs. It may be more realistic to attempt to get teachers with good ideas together with designers and programmers, who can translate the ideas into materials. In any case, I believe that the Utility will spark the creative imagination of many people, who will, in turn, create a whole new generation of exciting learning materials, leading to a higher quality learning experience for all those who use the Utility.

Finally, I would like to suggest another long-range potential of the Utility, one which is somewhat more elusive but of great consequence, if realized. The Utility could prove to be the focal point around which a new coalition might form to enhance the quality of education available to all citizens. That is, the Utility might bring together in common purpose a host of associations, agencies and individuals whose combined talents, carefully orchestrated, could change the countenance of education. Suppose this new coalition began by bringing corporations, teachers, associations, administrative associations, state boards of education, local boards of education and colleges of education personnel together to discuss how best to implement the concept of the Utility. And, further, suppose you added other groups to the coalition, such as educational researchers, continuing and adult educators, vocational/technical educators, philosophers and liberal arts professors. Suppose creative people and groups *outside* the education system, but with ideas for education, joined the coalition. And suppose each of these groups and individuals focused on how to make high quality, individualized education a reality? Why couldn't this coalition bring about a renaissance in learning?

I see this coalition already building. The Utility represents a positive approach to solving educational problems, at a time when we very much need such problem solving. People throughout this nation and, indeed, throughout the world, are beginning to sense a rebirth of educational optimism. The Utility just could be the vehicle for driving that optimism even further, to the point that the *practice* of education is irrevocably changed for the good.

The potential is thus great, but there are some pitfalls to be avoided. I'd like to point out some areas I believe will need to be carefully thought about as the Utility is implemented, for *how* they are handled could spell the difference between success and failure. I do not mean to infer by my remarks that AT&T/NIU have not *thought* of these issues but rather to affirm, from an educator's perspective, that the issues are of some importance.

One area of potential problems is in the technology itself: the system simply must work as it is supposed to work. The hardware must be functional, and the software and/or information must be available when it is needed. Maintenance of the system must be of the highest quality, with repairs made, when necessary, in a timely manner. Furthermore, the mechanics of the system must not be so complicated or mysterious as to alarm the average teacher, for if the system appears too complicated to use, it will *not* be used.

This may seem to be a trivial point. In the years I have worked as an educator, however, I can attest with some experience that the *mechanics* of many technologies, and *not* the validity of the conceptual basis of the technology, are what negate their successful application. It is the film that breaks, the projection bulb that blows (of course there is no replacement bulb), the cord that doesn't reach, the malfunctioning of the receiving dish outside the school building, the microcomputer terminal in the repair shop: the *mechanics* drive teachers and learners to abandon tchnologies.

The Utility appears considerably more complex than the film projector or even the television set. The Utility promises much but seems dependent on so many things working correctly, and at the right times. Some educators will be very nervous about the complexity, but most will be willing to give the system a try, even to let the system fail on occasion. But over the long haul, reliability must be there. If too many things fail, too many pieces of information do not make it to the learner's terminal, too much time is required to repair a broken monitor, too much of any of this kind of technological malfunctioning, the system will not be used. When you've spent time preparing an exciting program of study for 30 young people and the system does not permit you to deliver your plans, you develop a very long memory about such instances. Educators will be tolerant to a point. When that point is reached, a technology that does not deliver is headed for obsolescence.

Another area of great concern to educators (and learners) relates to the kind of information resources available via the Utility. Throughout this book, I have inferred that the Utility will make possible access not only to *more* information resources but, in time, to qualitatively *better* resources than currently available to educators. This is true particularly with regard to computing software/programs. I am convinced that the development of creative new kinds of educational programming needs to be of highest priority, coupled with the acquisition for the Utility of the best of the educational software currently available. If teachers find the Utility is merely the repository of uninspired educational programming, then the Utility will not be used. Again, teachers have *some* patience and will be willing to accept the fact that the Utility will not have, on the day it starts operation, a comprehensive collection of brand new, highly creative software for every subject field. But teachers need to see some progress, some commitment to getting good materials into the system. The major complaint from both teacher and learner about current microcomputer technologies focuses on the absence of adequate, quality software. The Utility cannot afford to continue current trends. A radical departure from business-as-usual is needed.

A third possible pitfall is related to the presence (or absence) of a clearly defined support structure for users of the Utility. In my judgment, creating a highly visible support structure is one of the things that will assure the Education Utility will be a technology that makes a difference in education. Conversely, I believe the *absence* of such a support system will condemn the Utility to mediocrity at best, and total rejection by the education community at worst.

What do educators need from a good support system? They need, first, a means of receiving training in how to effectively use the Utility. The Utility will make different kinds of demands on teachers. Few of us have been trained to use a technology of the magnitude of the Utility. We need to know where to go to receive training, and we must be able to take advantage of the training when it is delivered.

Second, educators need a source of *ideas* for how to improve their use of the Utility. There must be a place to call or visit to get help, share ideas, be stimulated. There must be a way to gain access to research findings and instances of exemplary practice. Educators must feel that there is an entity, or entities, that can be regularly contacted for new ideas or technical assistance. The *isolation* that is so much a part of many teachers' professional lives must be ameliorated.

Third, educators need to have contact with other educators who are trying to use the Utility. These contacts are vital if the teacher is to mature in his or her use of the technology. The contacts I am speaking of here are not the same as the contacts I've described, in Chapter Six, that the teacher might have with an entity such as the Academy of Learning Technologies. I'm describing instead the day-to-day, peer-to-peer contacts that are a source of both inspiration and support.

Finally, the educator needs the support system to acknowledge that he or she is doing a good job. All of us need such acknowledgments if we are to keep on going. Teachers who work with the Utility may need special recognition in this regard, for they will be blazing new trails. Some of those teachers will be out there alone, at least initially. They will need all the support they can get.

It is the *absence* of mechanisms designed to enhance the kinds of support services teachers need that will spell trouble for the Utility concept. If AT&T/NIU fails to recognize and creatively deal with these support needs, I predict problems. This is not to argue that AT&T/NIU must take total responsibility for establishing every aspect of the needed support structure. The two corporations could, however, send clear signals to the education community that they recognize the centrality of the support issue to the success of the Utility, and that they will work closely with other institutions in the education system to create the necessary support structure.

These, then, are my observations about a few of the potentials and pitfalls that are a part of the development of the Education Utility. My own summing up of these matters is that the potential far outweighs the pitfalls. In fact, the pitfalls are negative *only* if action is not taken to turn a pitfall into a potential.

I have attempted to write about the Education Utility as objectively as possible, but it should be evident to the reader that I find much to be excited about. It is, of course, much too early to know if the potential of the Utility in concept will become a reality. There are many things that could go wrong, or at the least, not as *right* as one might hope. But there is reason to be optimistic.

I began this book by saying I wished to describe a journey that was underway. I believe I understand the parameters of that journey a bit more, now that I am completing these last thoughts. The metaphor of a journey still seems to work. Each day, there is more visible through the rear view mirror, but the length of the journey ahead is not certain. What is painfully clear on this day is that the world desperately needs a journey toward understanding and peace. In the news yesterday is the account of a massacre at two airports. I am writing the first draft of these thoughts in New York. I have just come in from a very cold evening, and the homeless of this city are gathering wherever there is a hint of warmth. There is so much to be done in our world, so much inequity, pain, suffering. It is the holiday season, so there is also much joy evident in this city, and in cities and towns throughout the land. The contrast between pain and joy is so great at times like these.

Journeys are undertaken by some to alleviate pain, by others to search for joy, happiness, or fulfillment. The Education Utility is a journey toward understanding through education, joy through learning, and the alleviation of pain through the eradication of ignorance. The Utility represents a journey in search of equity. It is a journey that, for me, has held up thus far. There is a great deal yet to be done, if the concept is to take root in the reality of daily life in the education system. But the work is worth doing, the risks worth taking, because the payoffs potentially are so great. If enough of us work at it in an intelligent manner, and the idea fails, we will move on to the next attempt, knowing that we tried. But the idea should not be permitted to fail because it was not given a chance.

I believe the Utility deserves a chance. I hope educators will grab hold of the idea, mold it to fit, then make it create a powerful Learning Society. Oscar Wilde was said to have observed that "A map that doesn't include Utopia isn't worth even glancing at."

Let the journey continue.

REFERENCES

Boorstin, D.J. (1983). *The Discoverers: A History of Man's Search to Know His World and Himself.* New York: Random House.

Chisholm, T.A. & Krishnakumar, P. (1981). "Are Computer Simulations Sexist?" *Simulation & Games,* 12 (4), 379-392.

Cleveland, H. (1985). "Educating for the Information Society." *Change,* 17 (4), 13-21. (July/August).

Collis, B. (1985). "Sex Differences in Secondary School Students' Attitudes Toward Computers." *The Computing Teacher,* 12 (7), 33-36.

Cornish, E. (1983). "The Future of Jobs." *Careers Tommorow: The Outlook for Work in a Changing World.* Bethesden, MD: World Future Society.

Cronbach, L.J., & Snow, R.F. (1977). *Aptitudes and Instructional Methods.* New York: Irvington Press.

Demetrulias, D.M. (1985). "Gender Differences and Computer Use." *Educational Horizons,* 63, (3), 133-135.

Diem, R.A. (1985). "A Study of Children's Attitudes and Reactions to the New Technology." *Social Education,* 49 (4), 318-320.

Dunkin, M.J. & Biddle, B.J. (1974). *The Study of Teaching.* New York: Holt, Rinehart, & Winston.

Eurich, N.P. (1985). *Corporate Classrooms: The Learning Business.* A Carnegie Foundation Special Report. Princeton, NJ: Princeton University Press.

Fisher, G. (1984). "Access to Computers." *The Computing Teacher,* 11 (8), 24-26.

Gardner, J. (1963). *Self Renewal.* New York: Harper and Row, Publishers.

Gagne, R. & Briggs, L. (1979). *Principles of Instructional Design.* New York: Holt, Rinehart, & Winston.

Gilliland, K. (1984). "Equals in Computer Technology." *The Computing Teacher,* 11 (8), 42-44.

Gulick, L. & Urwick, L. (Eds). (1937). *Papers on the Science of Administration.* New York: Institute of Public Administration.

Haven, R. Instructional Software, 1984: Trends and State of the Art. Paper delivered at the annual meeting of the American Educational Research Association, Chicago.

Jeter, J. Chauvin, J. (1982). "Individualizing Instruction: Implications for the Gifted." *Roeper Review*, 5 (1), 2-3.

Johnson, D.W. & Johnson, R.T. (1985). "Computer-assisted Cooperative Learning." Unpublished Manuscript. University of Minnesota.

Johnson, R.T., Johnson, D.W., & Stanne, M.B. (1985a). *A Comparison of Computer-assisted Cooperative, Competitive, and Individualistic Learning*. Manuscript submitted for publication.

Johnson, R.T., Johnson, D.W., & Stanne, M.B. (1985b). *Computer-assisted Instruction: Influences of Cooperative, Competitive, and Individualistic Goal Structures*. Manuscript submitted for publication.

Joyce, B., & M. Weil. (1980). *Models of Teaching*. Prentice-Hall, Inc.: New Jersey.

Leukhardt, J.C. (1981). "A study of the differences by sex in self selection patterns of participation in activities of a progam for high school gifted students." (ERIC Document Reproduction Service No. ED 212 121).

Lockheed, M.E. & Frakt, S.B. (1984). "Sex Equity: Increasing Girls' Use of Computers." *The Computing Teacher*, 11 (8), 16-18.

Lucking, R. (1984). "Gender Differences in Attitudes Toward Computers." *Voice of Youth Advocates*, 7 (2), 80-82.

Miura, I.M. & Hess, R.D. (1984). "Enrollment Differences in Computer Camps and Summer Classes." *The Computing Teacher*, 11 (8), 22.

Niebuhr, H. (1984). *Revitalizing American Learning: A New Approach That Just Might Work*. Belmont, CA: Wadsworth Publishing Company, Inc.

Sanders, J.S. (1985). "Making the Computer Neuter." *The Computing Teacher*, 12 (7), 23-27.

Schubert, J.G. DuBois, P.A., & Wolman, J.M. (1985). "Ideas for Equity in Computer Learning." *The Computing Teacher*, 12 (7), 40-42.

Smith, C.L. & Stander, J.M. (1981). "Human Interaction with Computer Simulation." *Simulation & Games*, 12 (3), 345-360.

Tobias, S. (1981). "Adapting Instruction to Individual Differences Among Students." *Educational Psychologist*, 16, 111-120.

Turkle, Sherry. (1984). *The Second Self: Computers and the Human Spirit*. New York: Simon and Schuster, Inc.

Index

DENNIS D. GOOLER

Dennis D. Gooler was born in Minnesota, and spent his early years in International Falls. He received his baccalaureate and masters degrees from the University of Minnesota, and his doctorate in Educational Psychology from the University of Illinois. He was a junior high school teacher of English and Social Studies for several years, prior to completing his doctorate. His first professorial appointment was at Syracuse University, where he also served as Chair of the Department of Instructional Technology. Dr. Gooler also served for several years as the Director of Research and Evaluation for the University of Mid-America. He served as Dean of the College of Education at San Diego State University, prior to his current appointment as Dean of the College of Education at Northern Illinois University.